MODERN CULTURE AND WELL-BEING

MODERN CULTURE AND WELL-BEING

Towards a Sustainable Future

EDITED BY CATHERINE CONLON

Published 2020 by
Veritas Publications
7–8 Lower Abbey Street
Dublin 1, Ireland
publications@veritas.ie
www.veritas.ie

ISBN 978 1 84730 908 2

10 9 8 7 6 5 4 3 2 1

A catalogue record for this book is available from the British Library.

Designed by Clare Meredith, Veritas Publications
Cover design by Jeannie Swan, Veritas Publications
Printed in the Republic of Ireland by SPRINT-print Ltd, Dublin

Veritas books are printed on paper made from the wood pulp of managed forests. For every tree felled, at least one tree is planted, thereby renewing natural resources.

CONTENTS

SECTION FOUR

SUSTAINABILITY

SECTION FIVE

SELFISHNESS, ALTRUISM AND RESILIENCE

SECTION SIX

THE WAY FORWARD

INTRODUCTION

Some of my earliest memories are of time spent on a small farm in Kilnamona, four miles outside Ennis, in Co. Clare. I remember my uncle putting me up on a horse that ploughed a furrow for the seeds that would become crops to be harvested in the autumn.

I remember waking up very early in the dark and joining him in the cow shed where he taught me to hand milk the cows. I remember the tiny fluffy chickens – only recently hatched – and hens skittering across the kitchen floor. A haggard full of vegetables. Feeding piglets with scraps and leftovers. Long days in the fields, always sunny, on top of haystacks as they were pitchforked into shape and tied down with string, and rainy days spent indoors playing cards.

While this picture is instantly recognisable to children who grew up in Ireland forty years ago, this type of rich pastoral experience no longer exists in modern Ireland.

The twenty-first century is, for many, a time of unprecedented material comfort and choice, free of the diseases and social constraints that existed in previous centuries. Improvements in sanitation, housing, healthcare, social welfare and education have all transformed the world in which we live, while more recent advances in computer technology, tablets and electronic devices mean that we have global data at our fingertips.

The Millennium Development Goals Report 2015 stated that the number of people living in extreme poverty fell by more than half, from 1.9 billion in 1990 to eight hundred and thirty-six million in 2015; while the number of people in the working middle class, living on more than $4 per day, has almost tripled between 1991 and 2015, making up half the work force in developing countries. Child mortality has declined by more than half, dropping from ninety to forty-three deaths per thousand between 1990 and 2015.

Life expectancy in Ireland has increased by thirty years in the last century. Average life expectancy in 1916 was fifty-three whereas it is now well over eighty for both men and women. This reflects improvements in vaccinations and treatments for infectious diseases, including tuberculosis, as well as widespread improvements in infant mortality, maternal mortality and the prevention and treatment of chronic disease.

Despite these extraordinary achievements, there is a profound malaise at the core of modern society, as evidenced by the prevalence of mental ill-health, obesity and the unacceptable scourge of homelessness. In this modern world, consumer choice has mushroomed to the extent that materialism pervades all aspects of life. At the same time, social inequality has never been more pronounced. The cost of housing in major urban centres has rocketed to the point that only the wealthiest in society can afford to own property, exasperating problems of homelessness in major cities. Drug abuse and alcoholism are pervasive in every town and village. Shared cultural systems, both religious and societal, have been questioned and found wanting. With long working days, taxing commutes and exorbitant childcare costs, many parents – overworked and overwhelmed – are often left wondering: what is it all for?

A surfeit of food, alcohol, material goods and technology in affluent societies brings its own problems: too much food, laden with sugar, fat, salt and preservatives; much too much screen time; little rest; little cherishing of the soul. On top of all this we are now faced with the crisis of global warming, ecological devastation, loss of biodiversity and a requirement to cut carbon dioxide emissions – resulting from fossil-fuel consumption and intensive agriculture – to zero in the next thirty years or risk collapse of the social infrastructures we have refined in recent decades.

But there is room for hope.

It is from the most creative parts of humanity that solutions to the most profound problems emerge. The Irish are known across the globe for their creativity and generosity. The time has come for innovative, imaginative and ethical decisions to be taken to bring us forward from the brink of ecological and societal collapse to a new era of sustainability and collective inclusiveness.

This book will explore the aspects of contemporary living that influence the way we feel, the way we eat and move, the addictive traits that consume us, as well as factors in our lives that have resulted in the exponential rise in fossil-fuel consumption and ecological devastation that now threaten to overwhelm the entire planet.

I sought out experts in the fields of mental well-being, human health and nutrition, addiction, politics, sociology, sustainability and public health to contribute their viewpoints on the origins of these subjects in our culture. More importantly I asked the contributors to share their views on what we need to do, individually and collectively, to move towards inhabiting a better world and creating a sustainable future, both for ourselves and for the generations that will follow.

The book has been divided into six parts. Section one explores the relationship between modern culture and well-being in its broadest sense, while subsequent sections hone in on the most salient features at play when it comes to physical and mental health in Ireland today: Diet and Exercise; Addiction; Sustainability; Selfishness and Altruism; and The Way Forward.

Modern Culture and Well-being

In the first chapter, Patricia Casey discusses the degree to which psychiatric illness is preventable, as well as exploring the benefits of active coping, a healthy lifestyle and other practices that will help to build resilience, the corner stone of well-being.

Breda O'Brien, in a timely consideration of how to best nurture our children, considers how 'we seem to have stumbled into the worst model of parenting imaginable – always present physically, thereby blocking children's autonomy, yet only fitfully present emotionally.' It is reported that the continuing 'partial' attention of adults is in fact more damaging than a historical model that often saw children being left to their own devices in terms of play and personal development. Tony Humphreys explores the sad reality of fear as a dominant factor in most people's lives, while Joan Freeman considers one of the most common causes for concern among young people today: social media. The Pieta House founder ponders how filtered images imposed on screen by peers can lead to a crippling burden of excessive expectations, harsh inner criticism and a futile quest for perfectionism.

Diet and Exercise

Although the relationship between nutrition, fitness and health – both physical and mental – has never been better understood than in the twenty-first century, it's ironic that poor diet and exercise continue to afflict vast swathes of society. Donal O'Shea explores the reasons why this is the case in a chapter highlighting the overriding environmental factors that influence obesity – these include food production, advertising, physical activity infrastructure and the work environment.

Cliodhna Foley-Nolan expands on this, as she discusses the ubiquitous nature of energy-dense snack foods, along with the relentless marketing of these foods by the food industry, underpinning the global epidemic of obesity; she also offers some practical solutions to the over-availability and over-marketing of these highly processed products. William Reville examines the link between the obesogenic environment and sustainability, acknowledging that food production contributes 24% of warming greenhouse gas emissions and accounts for 70% of freshwater use, as well as being the main driver of biodiversity loss. He considers ways in which food production can change to drive down obesity and enhance sustainability.

Addiction

The pressures and expectations placed upon people in the modern world can often manifest itself in addiction of various forms. Colin O'Gara discusses the influence of stress globally and its impact on addiction in all its guises – alcohol, benzodiazepines, prescription medication, stimulants, designer drugs, gambling, pornography – as well as body image issues fuelling addiction to anabolic steroids, supplements and dieting. He examines the culture of overworking that exists in multinational organisations and the degree to which this facilitates addictive behaviours.

Sustainability

John Gibbons explores biodiversity loss in the modern world. He states that since 1970 around two thirds of all wild and land animals have disappeared, that the oceans have become 30% more acidic since 1950 and that the global population of sea birds has declined by 70%. Widespread and rapid collapse of insect populations has occurred

In the same period, levels of atmospheric carbon dioxide have increased by nearly 40% to the highest levels in at least three million years. Ireland's carbon footprint is high, thirteen tonnes per person, 45% higher than the EU average. The emissions in the transport and agriculture sector continue to climb. Compared to EU models of high quality, high frequency and low cost public transport, allied with safe pedestrian and cycling infrastructure, Ireland's transport policy has focused on road and motorway building, a policy influenced heavily by lobbying from industry.

Agriculture is Ireland's number one source of greenhouse gas emissions, influenced by an industry weighted heavily towards the beef and dairy sector. Despite investment in the promotion of Irish agriculture as both 'natural' and 'sustainable', Gibbons quotes a 2017 EU Commission report as stating that it is neither.

Alan Mathews discusses options for reduction of agricultural emissions. Despite improved carbon efficiency in recent years, overall agricultural output has increased at an even faster rate, so that absolute levels continue to rise. Additional efforts are required. This may include forestry, 're-wetting' of peatlands, use of energy crops and agroforestry, as well as greater provisions of ecosystems such as biodiversity and flood management and a reduction in ruminant animals.

Maria Kirrane considers the human influences on declining insect populations, while Conor Faughnan and Eamon Ryan expound on the need to revolutionise our transport systems for clean and sustainable transport policy.

John Sweeney discusses the deeply entrenched concept in the western psyche that growth is good, growth is inevitable and that growth equates with economic and social progress. The dominance of this economic paradigm, to the exclusion of ethical concerns for the next generation and even for the other lifeforms that we share the planet with, is overwhelming.

Gross Domestic Product has been used as a surrogate for the health of an economy. A more sophisticated instrument, the National Welfare Index, incorporates social and environmental concerns with conventional economic assessments. In an era of increasing income inequality and environmental damage, newer tools are needed to monitor well-being and sustainability along with economic growth.

Selfishness and Altruism

The degree to which profit is more important than the potential harm that achieving that profit does to the area in which organisations operate is examined. Specifically, the ability of industries and companies to influence governments to modify laws to meet their own needs and maximise profit, is considered. Examples include: the tobacco industry; the processed foods industry; the coal industry with its link to acid rain; the role of chlorofluorocarbons in the depletion of the ozone layer; and the link between fossil fuels and global warming.

A key ingredient for cooperation and understanding to flourish between communities is education. But educational systems tend to focus on skills such as language, maths, discipline, success and work ethic, rather than the key skills involved in achieving self-confidence, health and meaningful relationships. These skills include building resilience, psychological flexibility and emotional intelligence.

Imagine the transformational attitude change that could potentially emerge if the education system focused on psychological and mental flexibility and emotional balance as well as understanding the interdependence of human beings.

Inequality too is a driver of mental and physical ill-health, obesity, drug addiction and violence. It also slows growth and triggers financial crises because low-income families cannot invest in education and health. Conversely, solidarity benefits the poor but also benefits the middle and wealthy classes who fare better with reduced disparity.

Davie Philips discusses the concept of strengthening resilience in a changing society. He examines the ability of social communities, that focus on ecological and human values, to build communities and transform local economies. These communities are challenging the dominant narrative of extreme competition and individualism by finding new ways of innovating, doing, thinking and organising that benefit the economy and elevates well-being.

William O'Halloran reinterprets what it means to be human – to think of ourselves not as destroyers but as creators. To create spaces that allow us to live in harmony with the natural world. Specifically, he considers integrating wildness back into places that have been used as resources for other purposes, such as housing, transport and industry.

The Way Forward

And so to the way forward. Shari McDaid suggests that collective action is needed to reshape society to one that fosters flourishing and affirms the equal value of all human beings.

Liam Lysaght considers the concept of ecosystem services, stressing the value of ecological processes that we take for granted such as purified water, soil health, climate regulation, carbon sequestration, as well as pollination and pest control – all of which are crucial to society and to a robust economy. He considers some key policy steps that would have a huge benefit for biodiversity.

Ivan Perry and Kieran Keohane affirm this view while highlighting the inter-related issues of economism, materialism and consumerism, as well as the over-emphasis on individualism. Ivan Perry suggests that it is increasingly clear that if we are to limit the harms from climate change and promote health and well-being, we need broadly based movements that are grounded in science and have the capacity to engage individuals and communities at the level of the beautiful and the good.

Fred Powell argues that if the world is to remain a sustainable planet, fit for human habitation, it will need citizens to produce a counter-narrative of an ethical civil society, based on civic virtue, social justice and democracy. This is the theory of 'double movement' – a titanic struggle between the push for self-regulating markets and the push back for social rights, multiculturalism and democracy – as the ingredients for a sustainable future.

He concludes by asking the question: should we despair or do we see hope in the future? The answer really depends on how we view the world. Do we understand it as a place condemned to eternal misery following the fall of humankind? Of do we believe that through civic responsibility it is possible to create a decent society, based on the values of social justice and equality.

Hope must be our inspiration for the future because without it we have no purpose. Hope is salvation.

I would like to think that the climate change and biodiversity crisis which threatens to overwhelm us is an opportunity to retrieve those elements of our past that were good; the times we lived in harmony with our communities and the natural world we depended on for our survival. That bucolic existence on the family farm was harsh and demanding, but, in many ways, everything was just as it should be. Nothing was wasted or thrown away and the land was valued as a resource that needed to be minded, respected and cared for. Immersing ourselves in our natural world is a vital part of our well-being and respecting it is crucial for our continued existence.

SECTION ONE

MODERN CULTURE AND WELL-BEING

As I remember, the film was called *Scaramouche*, but it may well have been some other black and white swashbuckling epic. I don't remember anything else about it, but one scene has stayed with me over forty years. The hero was a young and foppish French aristocrat who had been wronged in some way, and now had to learn to fight. He went to an old swordsman to take lessons. The old man's lines are the ones I remember: 'A sword in your hand is like a bird. Hold it too loosely and it will fly away. Hold it too tightly and you will strangle it.'

The lines stuck with me because they say something about happiness. We need, as human beings, things to hold onto. We need goals, ambitions and dreams. We need sex and love and affection. We need ideals and values and beliefs. Without them we drift into the relentless succession of one damn thing after another. Instead of being a journey with a destination, life becomes a maze whose walls close in on us. We must hold on for dear life.

The trick, though, is finding the right kind of grip on the things we need. Holding on too tightly to specific ambitions makes the inevitable failures intolerable. Holding on too tightly to ideals and beliefs makes them curdle into rigid dogmas that have no place for life's contingencies and ambiguities. Holding on too tightly to life itself makes the inevitability of death fall like a constant shadow over its fleeting pleasures.

And so, I think of happiness as that bird in the hand, guarded carefully and closely, but cupped with a touch so delicate that its heart beats without panic and its breath comes easy.

Fintan O'Toole
(*Sonas: Celtic Thoughts on Happiness*, 2009)

MENTAL HEALTH AND WELL-BEING

PATRICIA CASEY

Mental illness and mental wellness are not two sides of the same coin but one. There is a continuum between mental illness (the presence of severe mental illness) at one end and mental well-being (happiness, contentment, etc.) at the other. Along this continuum there are those who are unhappy, struggling to function, who perhaps have social and financial problems rendering their lives difficult and problematic but who do not have a psychiatric condition; and those who have milder mental illnesses such as anxiety and depressive disorders.

We know that social factors like poverty, unemployment and isolation contribute to our overall levels of unhappiness and discontentment, while events that befall us in life also contribute. For some, the impact of these can be to trigger a psychiatric illness like depressive illness or an anxiety disorder; for others, the effect may be to cause frustration, unhappiness and discontentment, not amounting to a psychiatric illness. Others ride the storm and seem to cope, moving on with life and are generally contented.

What is it that determines which of the three categories above we fall into – illness (mild, moderate or severe in its intensity); unhappiness or contentment? Genetics, or our innate biological make up, is something over which we do not have much control. For example, if we are genetically programmed with a propensity to bipolar disorder or to depressive illness or simply to be worriers, it may not be possible to prevent that. On the other hand, if we have no such inherent risk, then we may weather the 'slings and arrows' that assail us; and if we are programmed to be of a relaxed disposition, then life, even with its problems, is much easier. Fortunately, most people, even those exposed to great tragedy and suffering, manage to come through without becoming mentally ill. While most may feel sad or disappointed or heartbroken, they come through the dark periods in their lives. They are restored and possess a sense of acceptance and contentment. Some even feel more fulfilled than before the event and believe that the events that have befallen them have made them more compassionate and sensitive to the plight of others. The ability of the human spirit to withstand these stressful events when they come our way is known as resilience.

Resilience, as a psychosocial construct, is generally described as the adaptive characteristics of an individual which allow them to cope with and recover from (and sometimes even thrive after) adversity. In light of the array of stressful experiences that are part and parcel of life, the factors that contribute to resilience are important to understand.

Anecdotal and research evidence from interviews with resilient individuals suggest that a constellation of psychosocial factors contribute to a resilient response. The scientific literature has identified neurobiological factors that appear to influence resilience, including our genetic makeup and also our neurochemical systems. Personality is also an important element and those with avoidant traits fare less well in times of stress. There is an understandable tendency to avoid dealing with problems and to hope they will go away. Rather than confront them, we often procrastinate. Those who confront the problem and deal with it have a far better chance of becoming mentally well again than those who only address the problem when crisis-point has been reached.

Self-help

Self-help focuses almost exclusively on what we have control over and helps us harness our personal strength so that the quality of our life is improved, both in times of trouble and in our everyday lives.

One of the more important self-help behaviours is to have time to relax and unwind, and to have time to give to those we love so that they, especially our children, parents and siblings, appreciate our love and respect for them. But if this is at the expense of time for ourselves then our emotional reserves will be drained. There has to be a middle ground between total giving to others on the one hand and complete self-involvement on the other. Healthy time in our own company helps us develop our reflective skills and critical skills, as well as enriching our spirituality and creativity. As the poet W.H. Davies (1871–1940) reminds us 'A poor life this if, full of care/We have no time to stand and stare'. So, taking holidays, going for walks (without headphones), reading and engaging in activities that empty us of worries will pay dividends.

Drinking in moderation and avoiding intoxicating substances such as cannabis, cocaine, etc., are part of our self-help and self-monitoring plan for staying well. Even moderate drinkers may increase their use of alcohol during periods of distress, but alcohol, a depressant, will worsen mood and carries the risk of abuse and dependence. So, vigilance is needed during these times. Our cultural attitude to alcohol in Ireland has fostered its tolerance to a degree that many other European countries would find alarming and so we have to take additional precautions to forestall this if we are overusing it to rid us of our worries.

Exercise also helps reduce the symptoms of stress and, even for those facing the usual day-to-day concerns, walking or jogging or playing sport releases endorphins, the biological substances that pain-relieving medications also release. For others, sport is a chore, and for these the distraction might be baking, listening to music, playing an instrument or reading, to name a few examples. The escapism that a good work of fiction offers is enormously beneficial. However, escapism can be excessive if it pushes one into a Walter Mitty-like world of total fantasy. On the other hand, a serious tome like *War and Peace* may provide helpful insights into the nature of humanity for some, or for others it might heighten their sense of despair. The choice is determined by personal preference.

Increasingly, social media is playing a bigger role in everyday life than was hitherto imagined. Much of what is readily available consists of inane 'conversation' or worse, emotion-filled outbursts. Some social media, especially Twitter, is unpalatable, angry, breeds prejudice and can incite hatred. Some point to the presumptive link between suicide and online bullying and are potentially a danger to life; others are dangerous to health, such as 'Pro-Ana' (pro-anorexia) chatrooms and websites. The benefits of meeting people with whom one has a shared worldview or obtaining support from boards linking people with a common illness, for instance, are evidence of the beneficial effects. Social media requires wisdom and self-restraint, though, with that caveat, it can be used positively.

More important, however, in maintaining mental wellness are the face-to-face relationships we form with our fellow men and women.

Social Supports and Networks

Human beings are social creatures and have a need for companionship and for love. It is accepted that having somebody or even more than one person to turn to in the face of stressful events is important. Being able to open one's mind and spirit to a trusted individual can help remove a burden. In listening, permission is given to cry, to describe frustration and to explore ways forward.

Loneliness, particularly among older people, places them at risk of developing a depressive illness. And even among the general adult population, having people to talk to, to confide in and from whom to seek advice is crucial for mental well-being. These social supports may be family members, neighbours, friends or colleagues. Having a shoulder to cry on is important, but even more important again is being able to obtain health-maintaining and positive advice. The benefits of support from others has been shown to be related more to being given assistance in practicalities rather than in being emotional per se. A kind word from someone is also worthwhile as it affirms that we are valued, respected and even loved.

Whether it be reading a book that their neighbour says helped them, or advice about exercise or about talking to a mental health professional, or simply just sharing personal wisdom, these positive guides can help a distressed or vulnerable person weather a storm which would otherwise have broken their spirits.

Above and beyond having individuals who care for you and in whom you can reliably confide, social networks are also relevant in propping up well-being. Social networks are defined as groups or organisations that form relations within communities. Social capital is a beneficial off-shoot from these, particularly when the networks bring a community and the individuals within it together with a common sense of belonging and shared purpose. These are important too, not necessarily to be receptacles for the problems of individuals within it but to act as a scaffold for very practical needs.This was the theme of one of social capital's greatest exponents, Robert Putnam. In his book *Bowling Alone: The Collapse and Revival of American Community* and his earlier related paper 'Bowling Alone: America's Declining Social Capital', the Professor of Public Policy at Harvard University pointed to the reduction in social intercourse that ultimately weakened the bond within communities which hitherto had enriched the fabric of those communities through civil engagement (Putnam, 2000; 1995). This he termed social capital. If people don't have a sense of belonging to a community, they become atomised and isolated. These ideas are encapsulated in works old and new. For example, the great metaphysical poet John Donne (1572–1631) wrote 'No man is an island entire of itself; every man is a piece of the continent, a part of the main'; while French writer Michel Houellebecq confronted the existential isolation of modern man with terrifying bleakness in his 1998 novel *Atomised*.

In the day-to-day lives of people, the absence of groups with whom one is affiliated - and individuals to whom one can turn for personal support - causes much suffering, while the opposite is enriching and enabling in dark times.

Active vs Passive/Avoidant Coping

Resilience is assisted by active coping. This is the process of psychologically and behaviourally facing problems and dealing with them directly. Passive coping refers to psychological attempts to avoid confronting problems or engaging in behaviours that will reduce tension such as drinking alcohol. An example of passive coping would be when a recently unemployed person does not bother to 'sign on' to social welfare or to look for employment, perhaps claiming 'there is no point' as 'jobs in that area are scarce'. A person who is actively coping would do both of these things, and may also engage in courses that will improve employment opportunities or do voluntary work to maintain structure and reduce the risk of unhealthy lifestyle habits developing. Training in active coping can enhance resilience.

Avoidance is one of the strategies that prevents healthy coping. While 'hoping for the best' may ward off here and now worry, it can deter the person from considering approaches and alternative solutions to the situation they find themselves in.

Pornography

Pornography is now in common use. It has been shown to be harmful to relationships. In general, it does not depict loving, respectful relationships but rather sexist, sometimes violent and degrading interactions between the individuals involved. Within most cultures and in the context of committed long-term relationships, it is seen as a sign of relationship dissatisfaction. Recent studies demonstrate that the more pornography is watched the greater the level of sexual dissatisfaction. The association appears to be that, for the most part, pornography builds up artificial expectations of the sexual side of a relationship, rather than that sexual problems drive a person to viewing this material as a kind of release from frustration. A recent study 'Till Porn Do Us Part: A Longitudinal Examination of Pornography Use and Divorce' found that initiating pornography use after marriage doubled the divorce rate among men and almost tripled it among women (Perry and Schleifer, 2017). The rates were higher among younger couples and among men who did not desist. Recent studies show that pornography use is an indicator of marital and relationship problems. This should direct those involved to seek professional help. Moreover, the depictions of sex in such material may lead to false expectations about the sexual act that impact negatively on the relationship itself.

Religious Practice and Spirituality

There is a burgeoning literature on the association between religious practice and mental well-being, in particular focusing on those who have major life stressors or who have vulnerability to common mental disorders. It is thought that the benefits of religious practice, shown in many studies, stems from the comfort and strength people draw from this. In other words, religious practice is actively helpful to those facing problems in their lives. This is known as the buffering effect. Those who disagree with this hypothesis contend that those who have mental health problems are simply too unwell to attend religious services, creating the impression that religious practice is good for mental health and that not practising is the reverse. The great wealth of scientific literature now available suggests that both of these explanations operate resulting in many people being able to attend church and deriving benefit directly from it, while others are deterred because of their depression or anxiety. But that is not the complete argument, as long-term studies show that religious engagement helps improve the outcome of these conditions also.

Another argument is that it is not religion per se that helps but rather having a wider community to offer support, or social capital as discussed above. Proponents of this view claim that being a member of a reading group or a football club would have a similar impact. Recent studies on the social aspects of Church attendance have shown that over and above this, religious practice of itself confers benefits. These include reducing the severity of depressive and anxiety disorders when they arise and improving the outcome with treatment. They also show that those engaging in religious practice seek treatment earlier for their illnesses, particularly for physical conditions. The evidence for this, based on many research papers, is discussed in *Religion and Mental Health* (Koenig, 2018). While this is most noticeable among those with common mental disorders, the effect on severe illnesses such as psychosis are much less marked. There is also evidence that religious practice assists with physical ailments such as recovery from surgery, wound healing and heart attacks. However, these findings cannot be extrapolated to suggest that religious people are completely protected by their faith from mental health problems, but that a level of assistance is offered.

How does this happen? It is suggested that belief in an afterlife and a sense of something greater than ourselves provides hope and solace during times of stress. Some activities such as prayer reduce heart rate, blood pressure and so on (BMJ study).

What about spirituality? 'I'm spiritual but not religious' is a common response to questions about religious practice. One of the difficulties about this response is that spirituality is a very broad concept and can mean anything from a belief that God is guiding one, to a belief in a force greater than oneself in the world, to seeing value in the energy generated by crystals. Some definitions, such as that by the World Health Organisation, are simply a statement of general well-being rather than of spirituality as traditionally understood, that is focused on the supernatural or on a power greater than oneself.

A book by the sociologist Wade Clark Roof published in 1993 made spirituality accessible to everybody. *Spiritual Marketplace: Baby Boomers and the Remaking of American Religion* described the recent shift away from traditional religious practices and denominational thinking to what some regarded as more personalised and creative ways of expressing spirituality (Roof, 1999). These included magic, angels, meditation, a belief in re-incarnation, holism and so on.

Studies that have explored this are challenging, particularly when some definitions are simply a statement of happiness. Studies focusing on people who self-define as spiritual have shown that this attribute does not make any difference to mental well-being.

Stability in Family and Personal Life

Our best preparation for adult life is our childhood and our experiences during these early years. We are not blank slates; we come with our genetic make-up, our nature, but superimposed on that is what we learn from our environment. Our parents in particular make an enormous contribution to the people we become later in life. The love and stability that we receive from parents and from extended family and friends, is the biggest contributor. The psychologist John Bowlby wrote about attachment theory in reference to the bond that forms between mother and baby in the early months and years of life. He believed that babies initially formed a single secure attachment, usually to the mother, and that from this strong base, others would form. If this attachment is disrupted or absent, then later relationships would be adversely affected also. For the young child, new attachments are formed with other family members and then with peers. At each stage, affection, respect and leading by example impact on the growing child and shape their view of the world and of themselves in the world. So, an affectionless mother will raise a child feeling unloved and potentially incapable themselves of giving and receiving love.

A child bullied at school by peers will grow up feeling fearful and believing that bullying is 'normal' unless it is promptly stopped.

Parents who are absent emotionally and do not respond to their child's need for love will have children who do not find attachment easy and they either become cold or aloof, or overly dependent as they crave the closeness in adult life that eluded them as children. And, of course, the opposite is true also with children who experienced love and warmth developing into caring, self-respecting adults. This is something of a simplification since various other events can intervene along the pathway from childhood to adulthood, but the preparedness for responding positively to such events has its roots in the early years of childhood.

Is Stress Bad for You?

There is such a phenomenon as normal or appropriate stress. For example, the breakup of a valued relationship, the loss of a job or serious physical illness all trigger emotions in us that are, understandably, negative in nature. Indeed, their absence would suggest some major emotional deficit. The symptoms could vary from low mood, tearfulness, sadness, anxiety, sleep to appetite problems and so on. Many of us can identify with this scenario. If our functioning in day-to-day life is affected so that we are unable to work or withdraw from social activities for a prolonged period, our stress will be having a significant impact on us. The duration of reactions like this can vary from a few days to months. For most, the impact on day-to-day living is usually short-lived, although the emotional pain can last longer, even a lifetime. Take grief for instance. In the initial months, the feelings of sadness and longing can be very intense, causing unexpected outbursts of tearfulness, sadness and loneliness. The feelings may be overwhelming. As time passes, these lessen, and pockets of enjoyment and pleasure enter one's life again. The ability to work and carry out day-to-day activities may already have returned, often because there is no choice.

For all of these stressors, the most important thing is to have confidants with whom one can talk. It may be a family member, a friend, a clergyman or women, or a counsellor. The practice of seeking a counsellor when awful things happen is common but may be unnecessary (provided one has a confidant) and possibly harmful. This is because our own innate healing processes are not harnessed. The analogy of picking at a scab that is healing naturally comes to mind.

Of course, some people will need professional help, but most of us can deal with what life throws at us.

When are 'Disorders' not Disorders?

Common mental disorders (CMDs) is the term used to describe anxiety, depression and stress disorders that are prevalent in the general population. It is said that up to 25% of us will have one of these disorders at some point in our lives. One of the difficulties that we face in evaluating the frequency of these conditions is that the threshold for diagnosis is now so low that a person with an understandable stress reaction, such as those discussed in the section above, could easily be categorised as having a CMD requiring treatment.

Indicators that you may have a disorder following a stressful event are that you experience ongoing insomnia, panic attacks, sadness, suicidal thoughts and get absolutely no pleasure from life. In this situation, you should consult your doctor who will consider these symptoms in the context of your overall life situation when evaluating whether in fact you do have one of these CMDs.

Summary

Psychiatric disorders probably cannot be prevented, except those that are triggered by our lifestyle such as drug or alcohol abuse. However, having confidants, using active coping to try and identify solutions, attending to our religious practices if we are so disposed and engaging in healthy lifestyles will assist greatly in building resilience, the core of mental well-being. Neither must we forget that stress reactions are often normal and do not need any assistance other than accepting their temporary nature as we respond to the troubles that beset us all at some point in our lives.

Patricia Casey is an Irish psychiatrist, academic, journalist and conservative commentator on social issues. She is professor of psychiatry at University College Dublin and consultant psychiatrist at the Mater Misericordiae University Hospital, Dublin.

References

Koenig, H. (2018). *Religion and Mental Health: Research and Clinical Applications*. London: Elsevier.

Perry, S.L., & Schleifer, C. (2017). 'Till Porn Do Us Part? A Longitudinal Examination of Pornography Use and Divorce'. *The Journal of Sex Research*, 55(3), 284–296. DOI: 10.1080/00224499.2017.1317709

Putnam, R. (1995). 'Bowling Alone: America's Declining Social Capital'. *Journal of Democracy*, 6(1), 65–78.

Putnam, R. (2000). *Bowling Alone: The Collapse and Revival of American Community*. New York: Simon and Schuster.

Roof, W.C. (1999). *Spiritual Marketplace: Baby Boomers and the Remaking of American Religion.* New Jersey: Princeton University Press.

MENTAL DISTRESS

BREDA O'BRIEN

Suicide rates among young women in Ireland are among the highest in Europe (Gallagher, 2018). As someone who has spent her entire adult life teaching teenage girls, this statistic is frightening. There has been a significant increase in levels of mental distress in recent decades, particularly in the last ten years.

And yet, it is important to maintain a sense of balance. Young people are also more self-aware than they ever were and more likely to have honest relationships with their parents. There are also lots of resilient young people just getting on with life. However, there is a cohort who are more likely to have higher expectations of themselves and much more likely to suffer from anxiety and depression. Are these individuals who are more fragile simply more sensitised to the culture and therefore harbingers of dangers that will become more widespread? Or will more young women adapt to the culture in positive and healthy ways as time goes on?

Many people, most notably Dr Jean Twenge of San Diego State University, have correlated the rise in anxiety and depression with the advent of the smartphone, this mini-marvel in our pockets that connects us to the whole world but may separate us from our essential selves (Twenge, 2017a).

Twenge has conducted research on US generational differences for over a quarter of a century. The idea of a generation is a social construct and those that fit the United States do not fit Ireland as neatly. For example, she characterises those who were born between 1946 and 1964 as Baby Boomers. This timescale makes great sense in the US, where it characterises those born between the end of the Second World War and the mid 1960s (see Strauss, 1998, pp. 30–58). This was a time of unprecedented economic growth in the US. Gross National Product doubled, real purchasing power increased by 30%, four-fifths of American families owned at least one car and home ownership increased to 61%. Cultural mores changed dramatically. This was the era that culminated in Timothy Leary advising thirty thousand hippies in San Francisco to 'turn on, tune in, drop out'. It was also the era when such ideals were roundly mocked and derided by more conservative voices. After the relatively stable 1950s, there was an explosion of student and race riots, assassinations of the Kennedy brothers and Martin Luther King, along with a revolution in music and literature. It was no nirvana for minorities or indeed for women.

In Ireland? Some people still refer to the 1940s as the Hungry Forties and they are not talking about the Great Famine of the 1840s. Emigration was a reality for thousands of young people in the 1960s and 1970s because the Irish economy could not sustain them. The culture that they left behind was cohesive and Catholic, even if in a somewhat stifling way. Many of the upheavals of the 1960s in the US only had dim echoes in Ireland and social change happened much later here. In the 1980s in Ireland, a ban on abortion was placed in the Constitution by two-thirds of those who voted. A few years later, divorce was rejected by similar numbers. In the current moment, decades of social change have been condensed into a few short years and the pace of social change seems set to accelerate still further.

If, therefore, the American categorisation of generations has so little relevance to Ireland, what then of Dr Twenge's generation which she has dubbed 'iGen', that is, those born between 1995 and 2012? The interesting thing is that the cultural trends she has identified have had an effect right around the world and most particularly in Ireland. We are one of the most globalised economies in the world and cultural change is both affected and driven by the arrival of personal technology. The penetration of mobile technology in Ireland is very high. The Deloitte Global Mobile Consumer Survey in 2018 showed that 93% of Irish consumers own or have access to a mobile phone. Thirteen per cent check their mobiles more than one hundred times a day; 68% of 18–24 year olds watch live videos or stories on social media on a daily basis (Deloitte, 2018a).

Our usage is high by international standards. For example, the same survey conducted in Belgium found that 84% of Belgians aged 18–75 own or have access to smartphones, compared to 82% for laptop users. While 96% of 18–24 year olds have smartphones, only 40% of them watch a video on their smartphone every day. However, in common with Irish students, Belgian students look at their phones seventy times a day and one in four checks social media in the middle of the night. For daily communications, they choose to send an SMS (7%) or use social media (78%), rather than using the phone to call (Deloitte, 2018b). Ironically, there is plentiful anecdotal evidence from parents and others that in an age of communication, many teenagers and young people hate making a telephone call and will do anything to avoid it.

It was Marshall McLuhan who coined the phrase, 'the medium is the message' (1964). In other words, it is not the content that a particular medium facilitates that matters the most – it is the changes brought about on a subtler level by a particular medium that are more significant; that is, the way it changes human beings.

Twenge's conclusions about the way young people are changing are a cause for concern. Her much cited article in *The Atlantic* is much more nuanced than the somewhat sensationalist headline – 'Have Smartphones Destroyed a Generation?' (Twenge, 2017b) – suggests. She says that growing up has been delayed, with young people less likely to want to learn to drive, a classic marker of independence in US culture, but also likely to drink and have sex later. Most parents would be devoutly thankful for the latter statistics but less thrilled by the fact that teenagers also spend much less face-to-face time with their friends, tending to 'hang out' online instead. Teens have much less involvement with clubs and activities. As Twenge asks rhetorically, 'So what are they doing with all that time? They are on their phone, in their room, alone and often distressed.'

Interestingly, Twenge says that the deleterious effects of social media are more noticeable among girls. 'Forty-eight per cent more girls said they often felt left out in 2015 than in 2010, compared with 27% more boys. Girls use social media more often, giving them additional opportunities to feel excluded and lonely when they see their friends or classmates getting together without them' (Twenge, 2017b).

The infamous acronym 'FOMO' (fear of missing out) seems to afflict girls more than boys, but boys are not immune. Anecdotally, there has been a rise in the amount of time adolescent and young adult males spend in the gym, which might be positive in one sense, but is often more about vanity than fitness.

McLuhan also had another thesis, much less well-known than his famous 'the medium is the message.' He also talked about 'Narcissus narcosis, a syndrome whereby man remains as unaware of the psychic and social effects of his new technology as a fish of the water it swims in' (Next Nature, 2009). In other words, we are like the mythological Narcissus, drugged and in love with our own self-image and condemned to loneliness.

This is quite a bleak picture and, again, it is important to remember that many young people are navigating this new world with grace and intelligence. There are those, too, who challenge Twenge's thesis, pointing out that suicide rates were higher in the 1990s (a point acknowledged by Twenge herself; Eyal, 2018b). Nir Eyal, who writes prolifically about new technology, also points out that Twenge's data only applies to the US. Eyal is the author of the bestselling book, *Hooked: How to Build Habit-Forming Products* (Eyal, 2014). While this might seem to render him an unreliable critic, in fact, in many ways he agrees with Twenge, particularly about the ways to ameliorate the worst effects of digital overdosing, of which more later.

However, while Eyal's belief that Twenge's data is specific to the US may be true of European countries with less usage of digital devices, it seems very apposite in modern Ireland. Another US trend is unfortunately also very visible in Ireland, even though it may be an area that is too new to calculate the long-term effects as yet.

What is the effect of continuous partial parental attention on children, particularly on young babies just learning to interact and speak? Children of my generation thrived on benign neglect. I roamed around a farm for hours on end, mostly to avoid doing the kind of work my own children would consider akin to slave labour, but which was a mild workload at the time – feeding hens, or calves, or bringing in cows to be milked. (Okay, I never neglected those tasks entirely and it was only the first one that I even deferred.)

But as another article in *The Atlantic* – 'The Dangers of Distracted Parenting' – by Erika Christakis, states: 'We seem to have stumbled into the worst model of parenting imaginable – always present physically, thereby blocking children's autonomy, yet only fitfully present emotionally.' Christakis believes that the continuous partial attention of parents, as opposed to the planned benign neglect of being told to go outside to play, is much more damaging (Christakis, 2018). Again, this is a gigantic social experiment and we will not know the long-term effects for some time.

However, it is likely to mirror the fact that as both Eyal and Twenge point out, the negative effects of social media appear to be dose-dependent. The heavier the usage of screens, the more depressed and isolated teenagers appear to be.

Eyal feels that at least part of the solution lies with parents. He advocates that parents should discuss limits with their children. He had a conversation with his own five-year-old daughter, who voluntarily set a limit of forty-five minutes on digital devices, a limit she stuck to for five years. Those of us who are parenting teens wonder how that will last during the teenage years.

Eyal has written an article where the headline summarises his thesis – 'Kids' Video Game Obsession isn't Really about Video Games. It's about Unmet Psychological Needs' (Eyal, 2018a). He perceptively points out that humans need three things to flourish. They need a feeling of competence, which is the need for mastery, progression, achievement, and growth. They need autonomy, which is the need for volition and freedom of control over their choices. And finally, they need relatedness, which is the need to feel like they matter to others and that others matter to them. Sadly, modern life is not giving much of these to children. A video game like *Fortnite*, where players can hang out with friends, build virtual worlds, meet challenges and partake in bloodless cartoon violence, meets many of the needs that are not being met in their offline world. Eyal challenges parents to find means of fulfilling those needs in the real worlds that children and teens occupy. But given the distractibility of many modern parents and the pressures that they are under, are modern parents equipped to fulfil those needs for themselves, much less for their children?

I would add another psychological need, which is the need to feel that there is a purpose to their lives, and a sense of meaning. However, Twenge also describes a decline in religious belief, which is not being replaced even by a sense of spirituality. She believes that this is the logical consequence of a society placing more emphasis on the individual self and less on social rules: religion, by definition, is about something larger than yourself. Perhaps that is also something that parents need to think about: at a time when young people never needed a sense of meaning more, sadly, they are least likely to have role models who find that sense of meaning in faith.

Breda O'Brien is an Irish teacher and columnist, writing a weekly column for the *Irish Times*.

References

Christakis, E. (2018, July/August). 'The Dangers of Distracted Parenting'. *The Atlantic*. Available at: https://www.theatlantic.com/magazine/archive/2018/07/the-dangers-of-distracted-parenting/561752/

Deloitte. (2018a). *Mobile Consumer Survey 2018: The Irish Cut*. Available at: https://www2.deloitte.com/ie/en/pages/technology-media-and-telecommunications/articles/mobile-consumer-survey.html

Deloitte. (2018b). *Mobile Consumer Survey 2018: The Belgian Cut*. Available at: https://www2.deloitte.com/be/en/pages/technology-media-andtelecommunications/articles/mobile-consumer-survey-2018.html

Eyal, N. (2018a). 'Kids' Video Game Obsession Isn't Really About Video Games. It's About Unmet Psychological Needs'. *Nir and Far*. Available at: https://www.nirandfar.com/2018/07/kids-video-game-obsession.html

Eyal, N. (2018b, 6 November). 'The Truth about Kids and Tech: Jean Twenge (iGen) and Nir Eyal (Hooked)'. *Nir and Far*. Available at: https://www.nirandfar.com/2018/11/kids-and-technology-truth.html

Eyal, N. (2014). *Hooked: How to Build Habit-Forming Products*. New York: Portfolio Penguin.

Gallagher, C. (2018, 6 November). 'Irish suicide rate for girls highest in EU, report shows'. *Irish Times*. Available at: https://www.irishtimes.com/news/health/irishsuicide-rate-for-girls-highest-in-eu-report-shows-1.3688028

McLuhan, M. (1964). *Understanding Media: The Extensions of Man*. New York: McGraw-Hill.

Next Nature. (2009). 'The Playboy Interview – Marshall McLuhan'. Available at: https://www.nextnature.net/2009/12/the-playboy-interview-marshall-mcluhan/

Strauss, W. (1998). *Generations*. 1st Edition. New York: William Morrow, pp. 30–58.

Twenge, J. (2016, 23 March). 'The Decline in Religion Comes Home'. *Psychology Today*. Available at: https://www.psychologytoday.com/us/blog/our-changingculture/201603/the-decline-in-religion-comes-home

Twenge, J. (2017a). *iGen: Why Today's Super-Connected Kids Are Growing Up Less Rebellious, More Tolerant, Less Happy – and Completely Unprepared for Adulthood – and What That Means for the Rest of Us*. New York: Atria Books.

Twenge, J. (2017b). 'Have Smartphones Destroyed a Generation?'. *The Atlantic*. Available at: https://www.theatlantic.com/magazine/archive/2017/09/has-thesmartphone-destroyed-a-generation/534198/

FEAR IS A CREATION

TONY HUMPHREYS

Fear is a creation, a solution; not a weakness, not a vulnerability, but an essential, powerful and ingenious response to threats to well-being. Indeed, fear is an attempt to find well-being in a threatening environment. The threatening behaviours experienced in relationships during childhood in homes, schools and communities arise from the unresolved fears of the adults who have responsibility for young people's well-being. The sad reality is that fear is generational – not genetic – and is a dominant factor in most people's lives. Depending on the nature, frequency, intensity and endurance of the threats experienced, the fears created will be creatively designed responses specific to the threats experienced. This reality is captured well by the Jungian analyst, James Hollis, when he wrote: 'What is unconscious in the parent is transmitted to the child and the child's unconscious response may remain a continuing block to a fuller life' (Hollis, 2005). Hollis could have added that, if the parent or child, later on as an adult, emerges into consciousness and fearlessness, then the blocks to their expression of their fullness will slowly and surely dissolve. More about that later!

Hollis could also have included the other significant adults – teachers, childminders, grandparents, aunts, uncles – whose unresolved fears from their childhoods impact on their young charges. There is a notion that the future of society lies with children, but as long as children have to survive the fears of the significant adults in their lives, the future of society will always lie with adults.

The ingenuity, creativity and specificity of the fears manifested in children will always be related to their story to date, as, indeed, are the fears of adults. Story is primarily about the nature of relationships within and between individuals. To truly understand and resolve the fears of children and adults, an in-depth and non-judgemental exploration of their lives to date is essential. Any hint of frustration, judgement, intolerance, impatience, comparison, frustration, labelling, irritability, aggression or violence will result in an escalation of the fears that are presenting. What is required is a non-judgemental examination, understanding and compassion so that a return to the fearlessness of the individual's true nature becomes possible.

How adult fears behaviourally manifest can take a heavy toll on children's expression of their extraordinary, unique and individualised nature. No adult, no matter what role he or she plays in a child's life, ever deliberately – consciously – sets out to block a child's living. Freud poignantly describes this everyday reality in the following lines: 'What a distressing contrast there is between the radiant mind of the child and the feeble mentality of the average adult' (Freud, 1960). What Freud failed to appreciate is that the source of the 'feeble mentality' of the average adult lay in their fear creations when they were children and these necessary survival responses have persisted into adulthood, because no opportunities for consciousness to emerge had occurred. So many adults have exclaimed to me regarding the adverse circumstances their children had encountered from their actions: 'Tony, I didn't realise what I was doing.' The word 'realise' is a powerful word because it means to see one's behaviour with 'real eyes', with consciousness, and with genuine sorrow for the unintended pain inflicted and the acknowledgement and compassion, too, by the adult for his or her own childhood suffering that had persisted and been exacerbated into adulthood. Such realisations will only occur when safe psycho-social holding is present and the suffering – child's or adult's – is seen as a path – not a pathology – to conscious well-being.

Adult fear creations can manifest in many behavioural ways – their purpose being to reduce threats to their well-being – but, unwittingly and unconsciously, in turn, pose threats to children's –

and, indeed, other adults' – well-being. The adult created protective responses most frequently encountered by children are:

- Demand for conformity
- Being the trophy child
- Being spoiled (everything done for you)
- Absence of affection
- Impatience
- Disinterest
- Physical violations
- Irritability
- Lack of eye contact
- No encouragement
- Bullying
- Dishonesty
- Work addiction
- Perfectionism
- Criticism of physical appearance
- Comparisons
- Substance addiction
- 'Put downs'
- Absence from home
- Marital discord
- Hostile marital separation
- No joy
- Passivity
- Sexual violations
- No play
- Aggression
- Loveless tone of voice
- No fond embraces
- Unrealistic academic expectations
- Be there for parent, not for yourself

Clearly, the list of possible threatening responses is endless. Certainly, the intensity, frequency and endurance over time are important considerations, not only in terms of levels of well-being of the children at the receiving end of these protective responses, but also of the adult who unconsciously created them for their protection when children and, currently, as adults.

The kinds of fears that creatively appear in children's behavioural repertoire in response to the above list of adverse childhood experiences are:

- Fear of not being loved
- Fear of failure
- Fear of success
- Fear of 'put downs'
- Fear of criticism
- Fear of judgement
- Fear of comparison
- Fear of 'not being good enough'
- Fear of physical violence
- Fear of sexual violations
- Fear of 'being let down'
- Fear of abandonment
- Fear of public speaking
- Fear of telling it how it is
- Fear of living one's own life
- Fear of examining one's own life

These fears are manifested through unconsciously designed behaviours that serve the urgent purpose of reducing the threats to well-being that are being regularly encountered:

- Over-pleasing
- Passivity
- Appeasing
- Shyness
- Illness
- Aggression
- Temper tantrums
- Emotionless
- Lack of eye contact
- Obsessions
- Compulsions
- Perfectionism
- Manipulation
- Nervousness
- School phobia
- School refusal
- Anorexia

- Bulimia
- Self-harming
- Addictions
- Depression
- Delusions
- Illusions
- Nightmares
- Insomnia
- Distractions
- Separation anxiety

Not only do the above-listed reactions (anagram: creations) have the purpose of reducing the impact of the adverse circumstances being encountered, they are also symbolic representations of the hurts being experienced. Examples of these extraordinary unconscious representations are:

Protector	Metaphorical representation
Over-pleasing	Please see me
Passivity	Absence of love
Appeasing	An appeal for patience
Shyness	The absence of love
Illness	The sickness of not being loved
Aggression	The blows to my presence
Temper tantrums	The frustration of too many 'no's'
Emotionless	No heart contact
Lack of eye contact	No 'I' to 'I' contact
Perfectionism	The invisible 'perfect' me
Manipulation	Having 'to pull' to get attention
Nervousness	Fearfulness of 'not getting it right'
School phobia	Fear of not being there for an over-attached parent
School refusal	'Refusing' exposure to threats in school
Anorexia	Starved of love
Bulimia	Sick of not being loved
Self-harming	All the 'cuts' to my person
Separation anxiety	Separation equals rejection

It is important to note that the particular symbolic meaning of a child's or adult's troubled and troubling behaviours may differ and it is only by exploring and knowing the full dynamics of the adverse circumstances that the particular metaphorical representation will emerge.

What emerges from the foregoing is that human suffering, paradoxically, is a manifestation of adverse childhood experiences and also of a creativity that seeks to maintain some level of well-being, albeit, at an unconscious level. But why unconscious? Hollis says that 'the problem with the unconscious is that it is unconscious' (Hollis, 2005)! However, I believe the *power* of the unconscious is that it is unconscious! How difficult it would be to have the daily painful consciousness of not feeling loved. Welwood believes that 'not knowing in our blood and bones that we are unconditionally loved is the source of all human suffering' (Welwood, 2006). The wisdom of maintaining unconsciousness is to keep hidden and buried the reality of that devastating experience. The most common creative illusion I regularly come across in my therapeutic practice is: 'Tony, let me tell you I come from a happy family.' Only with great gentleness does that illusion dissolve.

Human suffering then has three dimensions to it:

- Creatively attempts to reduce adverse experiences
- It powerfully and symbolically alerts to the threats to well-being that are currently present
- It is a creative pathway to all the aspects of one's true nature that lie hidden

If it is adverse relationships that pose threats to well-being, it is the converse of those sad experiences that pave the way to expressions of one's true nature – all present in the radiant expression of the child:

- Lovability
- Curiosity
- Patience
- Eagerness to learn
- Tenderness
- Fearlessness
- Daredevil behaviour
- Endless energy
- Persistence
- Spontaneity
- Not fazed by failure
- Not distracted by success

There exists a conundrum to creating the unconditional safe holding of the child or adult who is troubled and troubling. If the average adult has created 'a feeble mentality', where can the adult be found who is conscious of his or her unique presence, lovability, power beyond measure, independence and fullness? It is only this adult who can provide the psycho-social safety of unconditional holding, patience, non-judgement, empathy, compassion and awe for the child or adult who have hidden their truly awesome nature behind amazingly-built protective walls. Yet, the reality is that most well-being professionals – psychological, psychiatric, social care, medical, nursing – are not required to engage with the professional who will provide the psychological safe holding for them to examine their lives, so that they bring consciously lived and fearless lives to the individuals who seek their help. And what about the even more important professionals – parents, teachers, childminders, police, lecturers, sports coaches, spiritual guides, political leaders, whose unresolved suffering can have such an unwitting impact on their young and older charges? Continuing personal reflection is the *sine qua non* of professional practice and development – in all fields of human endeavour. Such conscious reflection requires ongoing psychological safety for it to slowly allow all that has been hidden to be revealed, so that the examined life becomes a life lived and a safe holding for others to maintain or recover the fearless expression of their extraordinary nature and potential.

Tony Humphreys is a consultant clinical psychologist, author, national and international speaker.

References

Hollis, J. (2005). *Finding Meaning in the Second Half of Life*. New York: Gotham Books.

Freud, S. (1960). *Psychopathology of Everyday Life*, A.A. Brill (trans.). New York: New American Library.

Welwood, J. (2006). *Perfect Love, Imperfect Relationships, Healing the Wound of the Heart*. Boston and London: Trumpeter Books.

MODERN CULTURE AND WELL-BEING: TOWARDS A SUSTAINABLE FUTURE

JOAN FREEMAN

The hope and yet bitter uncertainty that underscores Yeats' famous line from 'Easter, 1916', 'all changed, changed utterly,' is still relevant in the context of the ever-changing landscape we find ourselves today with regards to mental health in Ireland. On the one hand, we as a society have at long last begun to shake off the stigma surrounding mental illness. We have begun many much-needed conversations in the public sphere that have encouraged people to speak out about their mental health, whether at home with friends and family, at the work place, or on social media. On the other hand, however, some of the recent advances in technology that have come to characterise our modern times have brought about personal and societal pressures like never before.

Ireland has one of the highest rates of mental health illness in Europe, ranking joint-third out of the thirty-six countries surveyed in the annual Health at a Glance report by the OECD (The Organisation for Economic Co-operation and Development), with 18.5% of the Irish population in 2016 being recorded as having a mental health disorder, such as anxiety, bipolar, schizophrenia, depression, or alcohol or drug use (OECD/EU, 2018, p. 22).

In so many ways things have never been better. We are richer than ever before; we have had so many advances in general health, life expectancy, in education and career opportunities, and yet we are not all happy. How is it that as we break down each successive obstacle towards living an easier and more comfortable life, we get more and more anxious? Evidently, well-being cannot be measured by GDP alone.

Our modern culture, with its increasing emphasis on individualisation and material and consumerist goals, has come to be seen by many as a world of greater uncertainty, disconnectedness and social fragmentation. We are undoubtedly still the same human race, but we simply cannot adapt as quickly as the technology we produce. As many of the advancements that have emerged since the advent of our technological era have brought about major societal changes at breakneck speed, many of us have been left without the tools or resilience to handle these rapid shifts. With the integration of smartphones and laptops into our daily lives we have become increasingly vulnerable to major threats to sustainable mental health such as online gambling, addictive gaming, excessive exposure to violent imagery, porn and fake news, online bullying, invasion of privacy, and the sedentary lifestyles that come from hours spent staring at a screen.

We cannot deny the fact that it is our young people in particular who are bearing the brunt of these pressures. The majority of today's teenagers and twenty-somethings are 'digital natives' who have grown up swiping on an iPad before they can even walk. Ireland currently has the highest rate of suicide among girls in the EU, and these rates are rising in contrast to the general downward trend in other groups. Ask any psychologist about the most common sources of worry among highly anxious young people, and he or she will invariably point towards the same thing: social media.

Creating the perfect version of your life on Instagram can be a heady and intoxicating experience for young people. It allows users to project an image of the life they have always dreamed of. But these filtered images inevitably invite comparison with the equally glossy versions of their peers and can lead to a crippling burden of excessive expectations, harsh inner criticism and perfectionism. All this happens at a crucial moment for young people, just as they are forming their sense of self and identity, and the pressure can become unbearable. Switching off is not an option because social media apps are designed to be addictive. Our brains come to depend on the regular hits of adrenaline and dopamine, resulting in excessive screen use and disturbed sleep.

When young people do make the brave decision to reach out for help, too few are offered real support in this country. In 2017 there were no less than two thousand four hundred children and young people with mental health disorders on the waiting list for CAMHS (the Child and Adolescent Mental Health Service), and still to this day there is no emergency service for children or adolescents after 5 p.m. or at weekends (Mental Health Commission, 2017). These are conditions that should not be tolerated in modern Ireland.

What more can we do to protect our young people from the challenges that modern technology presents, before they reach crisis point in an already oversubscribed health system? We cannot simply shield them from these risks, technology of course is not going to go anywhere, and if anything, the role it plays in our young people's lives is only going to increase. How then can we integrate it in a way that is sustainable to our sense of well-being?

For me the key lies in schools and education. Teaching young people how their brain works and furnishing them with skills to be self-aware and resilient in the face of difficulties has the potential to fundamentally transform their sense of well-being. It is vitally important that we incorporate mental health into the school syllabi as early as possible. It is essential that teachers and schools receive more training on mental health so that we can teach children the language to talk about and monitor their own health, and allow them to articulate the problems they face without shame or stigma. By showing children evidence-based well-being skills and strategies that they can embed into their everyday life, we can teach them that well-being is not beyond their control, that much like their physical well-being, positive habits – such as technology-free times and zones, mindfulness, and self-soothing strategies – can have lasting positive effects.

Schools are also uniquely placed to play a vital role in identifying young people experiencing emotional distress. All children and young people should have access to counselling services and talking therapies within their schools so that they will be much less likely to end up in crisis care. Such an early intervention approach has been shown to be a highly effective support for troubled children who are experiencing emotional health difficulties. According to the British Association for Counselling and Psychotherapy (BACP), counselling within secondary schools has been shown to bring about significant reductions in psychological distress in the short term (BACP, 2015). Here in Ireland it could certainly reduce the waiting lists we have been seeing with CAMHS.

Another path towards resilience and well-being might, conversely, be found in technology itself. Although I have so far emphasised the risks technology presents to mental health, we nonetheless must not turn our backs on the relatively untapped potential for technology to support mental well-being. For young people in particular, technology is a natural extension of their everyday life, and this very familiarity could prove to be a powerful tool in finding new approaches to foster well-being.

The growing phenomenon of mental health and meditation apps such as Headspace points to the distinct advantages of counselling and therapies on a smartphone or laptop. Irish-based health tech company SilverCloud Health provides evidence-based online cognitive behaviour therapy (CBT) and is used by both Aware and throughout the UK on the NHS. Another rapidly expanding area is artificial intelligence (AI), particularly therapeutic chatbots that are programmed to discuss mental health problems. Even online gaming – that great nemesis of all parents with teenagers – can develop programmes that teach valuable lessons surrounding mental health. Some in the industry have claimed that the interactive nature of games can have a greater impact in discussing mental health themes than the more impassive interaction required for films or television series.

Many psychologists have found that apps can provide a private and unintimidating first step towards addressing mental health difficulties. Access and flexibility are key here, the user can dabble as much or as little as they like depending on their needs and the time and space they can allocate. The anonymity of such platforms can also break down barriers of perceived shame and stigma, particularly for men who are generally less likely to seek help than women. Moreover, an app can be infinitely more financially accessible than counselling, which is all too frequently accessed only by those who can afford it. Apps and programmes certainly cannot replace the value of face-to-face talking therapies, but given the current pressure on waiting lists in this country, using technology to help struggling individuals could make mental health services radically accessible.

Through my own experience in the mental health charity sector and as a legislator, I have seen how vital it is that the individual efforts of local communities need to be supported by government. Services like Pieta House, Jigsaw and Aware are there to provide support in moments of crisis, but more foresight and regulation is needed from government to provide people with the protection and tools needed to adapt to our modern society.

In December 2018, we introduced the *Children's Digital Protection Bill, 2018* to raise awareness around unrestricted access to websites that encourage suicide and anorexia, and to enforce takedown orders against ISPs and social media undertakings that promote these sites (Government of Ireland, 2018). This action is only the beginning of what is needed from government. We must also put more pressure on social media platforms to police violent content and to regulate the addiction-fostering strategies of content developers. Furthermore, we urgently need to legislate on the emerging mental health tech, particularly the privacy risks surrounding AI-driven therapy. We need watertight legislation to ensure that any app or technology content making medical claims goes through rigorous clinical trials.

A flourishing and sustainable Ireland is one where mental health is prioritised by government and society in general. Achieving well-being and positive mental health is a shared responsibility and requires a redirection of focus, not only by organisations and individual citizens, but also by public authorities. By laying the ground work for open conversations and the creation of skills that cultivate resilience, we as a nation will be able to face whatever challenges modern culture throws in our direction, allowing us to achieve happy, fulfilled and productive lives. We need to stop hoping for a happier, more sustainable future, and start creating it now.

Joan Freeman is an Irish psychologist, mental health activist and an independent politician who has served as a senator since May 2016. She is the founder of Pieta House, a national mental health services charity.

References

British Association for Counselling and Psychotherapy. (2015). *School Counselling for All*. Available at: https://www.bacp.co.uk/media/2127/bacp-school-based-counselling-for-all-briefing-dec15.pdf

Government of Ireland. (2018). *Children's Digital Protections Bill, 2018: Explanatory Memorandom*. Available at: https://data.oireachtas.ie/ie/oireachtas/bill/2018/133/eng/memo/b13318s-ex-memo.pdf

Mental Health Commission. (2017). *Report of the Inspector of Mental Health Services 2017*. Available at: https://www.mhcirl.ie/File/2017_AR_Incl_OIMS.pdf

OECD/EU. (2018). *Health at a Glance: Europe 2018: State of Health in the EU Cycle*. OECD Publishing, Paris/EU, Brussels. https://doi.org/10.1787/health_glance_eur-2018-en

THE INVISIBLE SOCIAL IN IRISH MENTAL HEALTH POLICY

SHARI McDAID

Despite international consensus that mental health difficulties are influenced by a range of social, economic and environmental factors, Ireland's national policy on mental health shows a consistent tendency to focus on interventions with individuals. In this section, I will consider how individualism dominates Ireland's national mental health policy and ask how mental health policy and practice could be approached differently in order to improve mental health outcomes across the population.

Ireland's mental health policy from 2006 to 2019 was *A Vision for Change*, the report of the Expert Group on Mental Health Policy (Department of Health and Children, 2006). When published, it was widely regarded as a progressive policy that reflected a more holistic and community-based approach to mental health services. It was also remarkable for espousing a 'population health approach', and set itself as a policy not just concerning so-called 'mental illness', but also promoting good mental health among the population.

The population health approach is particularly evident in chapter five of the policy, on mental health promotion, but also features in chapter four on social inclusion. In both chapters, recommendations are made that reflect the need to address the social and economic determinants of mental health, including addressing poverty and building social capital.

Nevertheless, if one looks at the entire content of the policy, one can see that the balance of recommendations revolved around changes to mental health service delivery. Only twenty-six out of two hundred recommendations specifically addressed improving mental health at the population level, and many of these recommendations were for mental health promotion programmes rather than structural changes.

In contrast, population health approaches focus on the ways that positive mental health and well-being can be fostered as well as on preventing mental health difficulties. The World Health Organisation (WHO, 2005) defines a health promotion approach as consisting of:

> ... actions and advocacy to address the full range of potentially modifiable determinants of health, including actions that allow people to adopt and maintain healthy lives and those that create living conditions and environments that support health.

Such an approach addresses not only the personal factors leading to mental distress, but also civil, political, economic, social and cultural influences. So, the WHO states that, 'A climate that respects and protects basic civil, political, economic, social and cultural rights is fundamental to the promotion of mental health' (WHO, 2005).

Specific areas of social life that contribute to good mental are health named by the WHO (2005):

- Social inclusion and access to supportive social networks
- Stable and supportive family, social and community environments
- Access to a variety of activities
- Having a valued social position
- Physical and psychological security
- Opportunity for self-determination and control of one's life
- Access to meaningful employment, education, income and housing

This approach was endorsed in *A Vision for Change* which states:

> Actions in this area target the population and focus on the protective factors for enhancing well-being and quality of life, together with early intervention and prevention of mental health problems ... (Department of Health and Children, 2006)

The Expert Group identified the need to address the structural barriers to mental health, including reducing discrimination and inequalities. Nevertheless, the preponderance of the Expert Group's recommendations related to service provision for individuals.

Is a population health approach to mental health relevant in a relatively prosperous Ireland? The rationale for taking such an approach is supported by research findings showing an increased risk of having a mental health difficulty depending on socio-economic status. It has long been recognised that people in lower socio-economic groups have a higher risk of mental health difficulties than those in the upper income brackets. In Ireland, this is supported by consistently high rates of admission for severe mental health difficulties among unskilled workers (Daly & Craig, 2018). Similarly, the Healthy Ireland survey published in 2015 showed an association between deprivation and higher levels of mental health difficulties, with 13% of people living in the most deprived areas having a 'probable mental health problem' compared to 5% living in the least deprived areas (Ipsos MRBI, 2015). The Quarterly National Household Survey of 2015 also found that self-reported levels of depression were higher for people from very disadvantaged – compared to very affluent groups – while unemployed people were twice as likely to report depression as those in employment (CSO, 2015).

Homelessness too has strong associations with mental distress. Irish evidence suggests that between 51–71% of people experiencing homelessness have a mental health difficulty (Mental Health Reform, 2017).

The 2015 Quarterly National Household Survey found that females were more likely to report depression than men, while the Healthy Ireland survey of the same year found that 13% of women had a 'probable mental health problem' compared to 6% of men (CSO, 2015; Ipsos MRBI, 2015).

There is much we can do to begin to broaden our focus about how to improve Ireland's mental health, to start addressing these social circumstances as a means to reducing mental health difficulties. For example, the recently published report on precarious work by the Foundation for European Progressive Studies (FEPS) and Think-tank for Action on Social Change (TASC) suggests that mental health difficulties increase with greater employment insecurity (FEPS & TASC, 2018). Among other research, they cite a UK study that showed young people in temporary jobs were 29% more likely to experience a mental health problem compared to those in secure employment (Thorley & Cook, 2017, as cited in FEPS & TASC, 2018). So providing rights to job security is likely to reduce the extent of mental health difficulties, as is ensuring an adequate basic income. Similarly, ensuring that people can access affordable housing could promote positive mental health and reduce mental health difficulties. With regard to gender, providing better protection against domestic violence and gender discrimination may contribute to reducing mental health difficulties.

If we truly want to reduce mental distress and increase mental well-being, more discussion is needed about this type of mental health 'intervention' – the collective action to reshape society towards one that fosters flourishing and affirms the equal value of all human beings. Mental Health Reform, the national coalition on mental health in Ireland, has long been advocating for these types of structural changes. The next national mental health policy would do well to give more prominence to action at the level of the social determinants of mental health and to building an Ireland where mental health difficulties are less likely to arise.

Shari McDaid is the director of Mental Health Reform, the national coalition advocating for reform of the mental health system. She is a member of Healthy Ireland Council, the national taskforce on youth mental health, the Disability Stakeholders Group and is on the oversight group for the review of Ireland's national mental health policy, A Vision for Change.

References

Central Statistics Office. (2008). *Quarterly National Household Survey Quarter* XXX 2015. Dublin: Central Statistics Office.

Daly, A., & Craig, C. (2018). *HRB Statistics Series 38: Activities of Irish Psychiatric Units and Hospitals 2017*, Main Findings. Dublin: Health Research Board.

Department of Health and Children. (2006). *A Vision for Change: Report of the Expert Group on Mental Health Policy.* The Stationery Office, Dublin.

FEPS & TASC. (2018). *Living with Uncertainty: The Social Implications of Precarious Work.* Available at: www.tasc.ie/publications

Ipsos MRBI. (2015). Healthy Ireland Survey: Summary of Findings. Department of Health: The Stationery Office, Dublin.

Mental Health Reform. (2017). *Mental Health Reform Submission on the Review of 'A Vision for Change'.* Dublin: Mental Health Reform.

Thorley, C., & Cook, W. (2017). *Flexibility for Who? Millennials and Mental Health in the Modern Labour Market.* Institute for Public Policy Research.

World Health Organization. (2004). *Promoting Mental Health: Concepts, Emerging Evidence, Practice.* Geneva: World Health Organization, Department of Mental Health and Substance Abuse in collaboration with the Victorian Health Promotion Foundation and the University of Melbourne.

SECTION TWO

DIET AND EXERCISE

I wouldn't say that processed food, ready meals and even takeaways aren't relevant to modern life, it's just that over the past forty years there are three generations of people who have come out of school and gone through their home life without ever being shown how to cook properly.

Jamie Oliver

OBESITY – ALONG WITH CLIMATE CHANGE – THE BIGGEST CHALLENGE FOR OUR GENERATION

DONAL O'SHEA

Current estimates are that 50% of newborns today will live to be one hundred years of age. It is primarily the improvements in maternal and newborn health, combined with the development of vaccines and antibiotics in the last century, that have delivered this staggering probability. Non-communicable disease is now the major driver of death in the developed world. The food and drink industry happily trumpet that we have never been living longer – so all must be good. Not true. The problem is we are living longer but with more years of chronic disease than ever before. This in turn feeds into a pharmaceutical industry that is crippling our healthcare budget with high-cost medications to treat the diabetes, cancer and heart disease that are being driven by obesity.

Obesity is now causally linked to over two hundred non-communicable diseases and there are over one hundred and ninety individual established drivers of obesity. The determinants of obesity are mainly environmental (food production and advertising, physical activity infrastructure, work environment, insurance claims culture, etc.) and account for the increase in obesity we have seen in the last forty years. If the drivers of obesity are mainly within the environment, then obesity should spread within the environment – and this has now been proven in large population studies. You are 70% more likely to become overweight or obese if a friend of yours becomes overweight or obese. This should not come as a surprise as many chronic conditions – including cancer and depression – spread within the environment because risk factors for conditions cluster.

Since the 1980s there has been a doubling of obesity at a population level but there has been 1,200% increase in the prevalence of extreme obesity in the same period. This, coupled with the understanding that weight gain is 90% irreversible for 90% of people, has to put prevention at the core of our societal efforts around weight and obesity. The phenomenal gains in life expectancy over the last sixty years are now being actively eroded by the diseases which obesity drive and make worse. We now know the list of diseases extend way beyond the obvious diabetes and heart disease to the likes of cancer, dementia, sleep apnoea and asthma. A further challenge is the stark socio-economic separation in the prevalence of obesity. By the age of three years, our less well-off toddlers are four times more likely to be obese. This is the same sector of society that is less likely to engage with the health services – either screening or treatment. If we don't address this we will simply grow further health inequalities over the coming decades.

What is remarkable is that there has never been more focus on health in society. We have never had more interest in fitness. We now have population separation – 10-15% of the population are fitter than ever – but the vast majority of our population is sedentary. This pattern has crept up on society over the last hundred years. We have gone from taking an average of thirty-six thousand steps per day to it being exceptional to average over ten thousand steps a day – the new target for health!

The industrial age has delivered a seismic change to our society – creating what has become termed the obesogenic environment. We now move differently and our pattern of eating and drinking has changed radically. Cars, tractors, and escalators have replaced horses, ploughs and the stairs. In some institutions flights of stairs even come with a caution sign – as a trip hazard. Much downtime is now spent online.

Our beautifully evolved hunter-gatherer genes are being regulated by physical inactivity and high fat, high salt, high sugar, highly processed foods available 24/7, every day of the year. This is delivering our new normal – it is now unusual (abnormal) to be a normal weight. Even taking personal responsibility does not appear to be enough in the face of the powerful food and drinks industry push to expand their market at any cost – even the cost of our children's health. All the tactics used by the tobacco industry to grow a large base of young smokers are being adopted by the food and drinks industry to promote sugar-sweetened drinks to our young. There is now the clearest evidence that consumption of sugar-sweetened drinks is linked to childhood obesity – just as there was for tobacco causing lung cancer in the 1960s. The response of industry now, as then, is denial, obstruction, fabrication and continued unashamed big budget marketing – specifically targeting the less well off, less educated sectors of society. The food and drinks industry opposition to initiatives aimed at improving health and educating the public is consistent and co-ordinated. Strong opposition to initiatives such as sugar tax, calorie posting, clear food labelling and measures at curbing harmful youth alcohol consumption is testament to industries' true goal – profit, market share and dividend above all else.

Along with the progress of the industrial age delivering the obesogenic environment, we have an increasingly globalised and secular world where social media reaches into everyone's smartphone from the age of five years. Targeted advertising – based on the last few songs on a subscriber's Spotify playlist or the last few websites visited – is now routine. This is hard for human nature to resist.

This is all taking place in combination with the steady decline of organised religion, creating what has become a perfect storm in terms of the obesogenic environment. Consumerism is encouraged and pushed while the mechanisms for supported self-restraint are withdrawn. The selling season for Easter eggs – January to May – is now longer than nature's own seasons.

While there is a socio-economic divide, the overeating and underactivity that cause obesity is a problem for all sectors of society – with no demographic spared. Addressing the problem will require a whole-of-society approach. Individual responsibility will be required but on its own is not enough. Governments and the broader food and drinks industry need to start working to change the environment. We need to make the healthy choice the easy choice – only then can personal responsibility be expected to change the lifestyle choices that lead to obesity.

Donal O'Shea is a consultant endocrinologist and national lead for management of obesity in Ireland.

FOOD AND US

CLIODHNA FOLEY-NOLAN

'All is not well' – to paraphrase Shakespeare, we are confused, anxious and often apathetic and helpless. Never was there more 'information' and opinion on what we should eat and yet we have global epidemics of overweight and diet-related diseases, such as diabetes and cancers.

First allow me to explain why I, a medical doctor, got involved in this issue. Most of my medical career has been spent as a public health physician dealing with lifestyle behaviours such as smoking and antibiotic use. Then, partially by chance, I moved into the area of diet and health because of the surge of concern about illnesses related to poor nutrition and sedentary lifestyles.

Initially, I naively thought of food in somewhat concrete terms as another lifestyle risk factor without truly thinking through all the aspects of how our culture and our individuality influences our eating behaviours. Food is such a basic requirement. It also has multiple complex interrelated facets: our social circumstances; our economy and our environment which all influence our eating patterns.

The social aspects of food are myriad. Food means basic relief from hunger, it signifies home and nurturing, it equates with celebration and reward for achievement. However, today few of us are truly hungry; we spend a lot of time away from home-sweet-home and often over-indulge in food and drink on a routine basis.

Calorie-rich, nutrient-poor foods often called 'treat' foods (biscuits, cakes, crisps, chocolates, sodas and sweets) now have a big place in our world. We adults reward ourselves with these on a daily basis often because they are more available to us than five minutes' peace or a leisurely bath or stroll. Equally, parents now report giving children daily 'routine' treat foods as a reward because once again they are marketed and readily available to us. These products are 'everywhere' – in our sports clubs, in our hospitals and in our 'sweet cupboard' at home. This makes their consumption a socially acceptable daily occurrence; they're no longer a real indulgence but they replace other foods and are a substitute for giving ourselves and others that bit of time and attention.

Our social circumstances greatly influence what we eat, with those in the lower income group eating less healthily, having higher levels of childhood and adult obesity and related diseases. The gap between the social groups is widening with the least advantaged having shorter life expectancy (up to seven years' difference) and developing chronic diet-related diseases in midlife rather than later life.

The life circumstances of those on social welfare mitigate against eating well. Living in cramped housing with limited food storage capacity and poor ventilation would not encourage anyone to cook fish or cabbage. Equally, the preponderance of smaller supermarkets, garage forecourts and takeaways in less affluent areas also contributes to the food poverty experienced by the socially disadvantaged.

In today's food culture, social advantage can also have its potential traps. The rise of veganism is not necessarily a welcome phenomenon health-wise. Veganism is a challenging lifestyle choice with inherent health risks if not carefully followed. Also the premium price charged for many of these modish foods is not justified in nutrient value.

Other food fads and fashions that are in vogue with celebrities and bloggers often lack any scientific backing and in the case of diets such as the ketogenic diet are unsafe except under medical supervision. The Mediterranean-type diet (high in vegetables, fruit, wholegrains, legumes and nuts) is the only diet prototype that has been shown to promote good health.

This dietary pattern forms the basis for Healthy Eating Guidelines (portrayed by the Food Pyramid or Plate) which provide advice and information on the variety and portions and proportions of the foods that have been shown to promote health and prevent disease.

Healthy Eating Guidelines come in for criticism as being complex and/or too vague. I think much of the misunderstanding here is in the use of the term 'guideline'. A guideline provides general principles and rules. Healthy Eating Guidelines are recommendations and should be used to steer our consumption patterns, basically leading to a Mediterranean-style diet model.

Many people today complain of being confused about what is healthy food-wise. This is totally understandable. Credible information sources such as government agencies have very stiff competition in the shape of charismatic celebrities. Coupled with this is the marketing of products such as flavoured yoghurts and protein bars and energy balls which although having some nutritious value, are often heavily flavoured with sugar and fat elements and sold at premium prices. This all conspires to leave us feeling befuddled and ultimately defeatist about trying to eat well.

We are bombarded with an overload of uncensored 'information' about food and health. We have opinion mixed with personal testimony mixed with quasi-science, mixed with persuasive commercial agencies 'selling' us their perspective on the issue. We ask Dr Google for advice, we indulge in viewing a profusion of available cookery shows and yet we often do not afford ourselves the time and space to cook. There is surely some irony in this state of affairs.

The food prescription for a sustainable healthy future for us as a society is not a simple fix. Nevertheless, I am proposing some solutions that should help. Some changes are needed in our readily-available food choices. The over-availability and over-marketing of ultra-processed foods must be reduced by changes in food production and public policy. Food industry can play an important part by reformulating food products and by responsible marketing practices. There is also the potential for taxes and subsidies which support healthier food choices for us. These measures should especially favour those on lower incomes who currently eat less healthily and have less real choice. We are expecting too much 'self-control' from our children and ourselves.

As health professionals and scientists, we should be more courageous and frank in saying things as they are. Nutritional science is evolving all the time but the basic truths remain. The art of communicating uncertainty together with certainty is one that parents and we, the science communicators, grapple with all the time. We don't know everything but we must effectively speak to the hearts and minds of society relating the clear principles of healthy eating that we know to be true.

As a society and as an economy, we must revert to putting a greater value on the food we eat. The respect and monetary value that many of our continental European neighbours put on good food has been diminished in recent times at home. Instead of relaxed slow cooking we are expecting meals in minutes. Instead of encouraging sustainable agricultural practices we are expecting to pay minimum prices for quality food. The old axiom 'you get what you pay for' holds true for food too.

I am not suggesting an unrealistic or fanciful approach to feeding our families and enjoying good food. It is important to be realistic. So convenience in the form of such foods as frozen vegetables, prepared salads, packets of nuts and yoghurts makes busy lives possible. The potential pitfall is equating convenience with a protein bar rather than an egg, a tomato or a banana.

It is important that we avoid the extremes prevalent in our attitude to food and eating today. Yo-yo dieting and food fads are neither healthy nor nourishing. Equally a helpless fatalism expressed as 'they change the advice every week' is negative and futile.

In conclusion, I'm proposing the 'good enough' approach when it comes to eating for health. Rely on information and guidance from trustworthy sources and rely on our basic intuition about which foods and in what proportions make for a healthy diet. We should enjoy our food so that it nurtures the body and the spirit.

Cliodhna Foley-Nolan is a public health expert, food and health strategist and health communicator. She is former director of human health and nutrition with Safefood, the organisation which provides advice on food safety, healthy eating and food hygiene for consumers.

DIET AND EXERCISE FOR HEALTHY AND SUSTAINABLE LIVING

WILLIAM REVILLE

We now live in unprecedented affluence in the developed world and we also benefit from the huge advances made by science-based medicine which has eradicated many diseases, once the scourge of humankind, from smallpox to polio. Longevity alone attests to the power of modern medicine. Average life expectancy in Ireland was 53.8 years in 1911. Today this figure is 81.7 years.

And yet we cannot say we now live in an age of widespread and vibrant good health. New problems have arisen, many centred on modern diet and lifestyle. Although eight hundred and twenty million people worldwide go hungry every day, overeating and sedentary lifestyles drive an epidemic of obesity and related diseases across much of the globe. However, the consequences of obesity would be significantly ameliorated if people took regular exercise.

Modern intensive agricultural food production systems are also degrading the natural environment. Reform of practices in this sector is urgently needed in order to foster a sustainable environment.

Public health campaigns encourage healthy lifestyles and environmentalists advocate environmentally sustainable farming and industrial practices, but these campaigns struggle to make an impact. In this article, I will describe the simple basis of a healthy diet and adequate exercise and suggest how best to encourage people to adopt lifestyles that are healthy and environmentally friendly.

What is a Healthy Diet?

There are few subjects on which so much confusing, albeit well-intentioned, information is publicly disseminated as the subject of diet. We are bombarded with prescriptions about what is good and what is bad to eat. Some foods are demonised, for instance, red meat is 'bad', sugar is 'bad'; and some foods are canonised, so vegetables are 'good', fish is 'good'. Such advice is often dramatically reversed – for example, throughout the 1960s and 1970s we were told to eat very little butter and to favour margarine instead, but in the 1980s it was announced that margarine is worse for our health than butter; we were long told to avoid eating eggs because of their high cholesterol content but are now told that 'an egg a day is ok' and even lowers risk of heart disease; omega-3 fatty acid dietary supplements were recommended to, inter alia, lower the risk of contracting prostate cancer, until a 2014 study correlated increased incidence of prostate cancer with taking such supplements. Such flip-flopping has damaged public confidence in nutritional advice. Nutritional science must learn not to immediately publicise every last bit of the latest promising research results but wait and see how reliable the new results are before cautiously recommending guidelines.

Nutritional information is now displayed everywhere. Every food on the supermarket shelf bears printed information detailing energy content (calories) and nutritional composition (protein, fat, etc.). Such information might enlighten someone with a degree in nutrition, but only serves to confuse the average person and to persuade them that choosing a healthy diet is a complex matter.

But the truth is that, for the average person who is not suffering from a defined medical condition, choosing a healthy diet is simple. I think the best definition of a healthy diet, certainly the most succinct, and supported by extensive mainline scientific evidence, was given by the American Professor of Food Journalism Michael Pollan in his book *In Defence of Food*: 'Eat food, not too much, mostly plants' (Pollan, 2008).

'Eat food' means eat a wide variety of natural whole food – meat, fish, vegetables, fruit, whole grains, legumes, nuts, etc. For example, neither potato crisps nor processed meat would qualify as 'food'. Eating a wide variety ensures one neither misses important nutritional ingredients nor overindulges in anything harmful. 'Not too much' means eating in moderation and not so much that you grow fat. 'Mostly plants' means mostly vegetables, fruit, whole grains, legumes and nuts. Swap the traditional large plate of meat and small side plate of salad for a large plate of salad and a small side plate of meat. Consider skipping meat altogether on one or two days each week.

No food is demonised by Pollan's advice and there is no need to take vitamin/mineral supplements, with one exception – women who could become pregnant should take a folic acid supplement.

The Obesity Problem

We must eat to live. We eat food both to provide the energy (calories) necessary to keep our body cells working, to allow us to move about in the world and also to provide the chemical raw materials necessary to replace parts of the body worn out by wear and tear. If we overeat, that is ingest more food calories than we burn up, the excess calories are stored in the body as fat. Unfortunately, overeating is now so widespread that the world is confronted with an epidemic of obesity and its attendant diseases – diabetes, heart disease, stroke, osteoarthritis and more.

Seventy per cent of Irish males and 52% of Irish females now exceed their normal weight and 25% of Irish adults overall are classified as obese. Twenty-five per cent of Irish children are overweight. Obesity accounts for at least two thousand five hundred deaths per year and if current trends continue, obesity could soon overtake smoking as the single biggest cause of early death, diminished quality of life and increased healthcare costs.

Exercise

With use, mechanical machines wear out, but the human body grows stronger. As Herman Pontzer remarked, 'unlike our great ape cousins, humans require high levels of physical activity to be healthy' (Pontzer, 2019). We can strengthen our skeletal muscles by doing resistance exercises, e.g. lifting weights, and aerobic activities (walking, running, cycling, swimming, rowing, skiing, aerobic dancing, etc.) as well as exercise can strengthen our hearts, lungs and our general constitution.

Taking up aerobic exercise, regardless of age, weight or athletic ability, is probably the single most useful step you can take to improve your general well-being. Much evidence shows that regular aerobic exercise: (A) reduces your risk of contracting obesity, heart disease, high blood pressure, type 2 diabetes, stroke and certain cancers; (B) increases stamina, fitness and strength; (C) tunes the immune system, improving resistance to colds and flus; (D) helps to manage chronic conditions, e.g. reduces pain and improves function in people with arthritis; (E) strengthens the heart and keeps arteries clean; (F) counters depression and improves quality of sleep; (G) helps keep you active and independent into old age; (H) extends longevity.

Walking and running are the commonest aerobic exercises. Fortunately, really intense aerobic exercise is not required to derive maximal health benefit. Maximal fitness and health benefit can be achieved by walking four kilometres in under thirty-eight minutes six times a week or running 3.2 kilometres in less than twenty minutes five times a week. If you start out unfit you must gradually work up to this level. Exercising more will further increase aerobic fitness, perhaps desirable if you are a competitive athlete, but will bring no further health benefits and will likely cause knee, hip or ankle problems to develop over time.

Body mass is a balance between build-up and breakdown. In the prime of adulthood build-up and breakdown are in balance but after middle age breakdown begins to exceed build-up and muscle is slowly lost. If this loss is not countered it can limit ability to perform routine activities. Body flexibility also decreases after middle age. Regular resistance exercise (three times a week) is the best way to counter muscle loss – lifting weights, pulling against resistance bands, moving parts of body against gravity, etc. Stretching exercises will restore flexibility.

Losing Weight

As we all know, it is easy to gain weight but difficult to lose it again. Crash dieting to lose weight is ineffective. You quickly shed a kilo or two but your body chemistry soon senses your reduced food intake and adjusts metabolic mechanisms to slow the burning of stored calories. By now food cravings have intensified while enthusiasm for dieting dies away as weight loss slows down. Most people give up struggling and stop dieting.

Aerobic exercise is often recommended to reduce weight but, on its own, is not effective. Aerobic exercise makes our body chemistry work smarter and better, redirects the way in which we burn calories and is very good for health. But an aerobically active person will not necessarily burn off more calories than a sedentary person.

The most effective way to lose weight is to gradually reduce food calorie intake. This will produce a sustainable weight loss over weeks and months. This plan works best when accompanied by vigorous aerobic exercise, which not only tones the body but also reduces appetite.

In summary, you diet to control your weight and you exercise to improve your health. Pollan's advice on a healthy diet can be expanded to cover an overall healthy lifestyle: *'Eat food, not too much, mostly plants, and take plenty of aerobic exercise.'*

Why Do People Eat So Much Nowadays?

There is one particular reason why our basic biology is 'out of sync' with the modern world. Throughout most of human evolutionary history, food was hard to get; we ate it when we could get it and our body chemistry evolved to hoard ingested calories and to burn them carefully to extract maximum value. But nowadays, tasty energy-dense foods are cheap and widely available, marketed intensively; nutritional advice is confusing and work practices are either sedentary or call for little mobility. This complex of factors is termed the 'obesogenic environment'. Appetite for food is a primary human drive, even stronger than desire for sex, so nowadays many of us succumb to the temptation to eat a lot, simply because we can so easily do so.

Eating food anytime and anywhere was never easier than it is nowadays. Our cities and towns are festooned with fast-food outlets that target modern individualism and busy lifestyles with 'grab-n-go' tasty and calorie-dense hamburgers, fries, pizzas, sandwiches, sugary drinks and so on. You can even sit on your living room couch and use your mobile phone to order fast food delivered to your front door. And while waiting for delivery you can whet your appetite watching one of the many cookery programmes that are perpetually showing on TV. While there is nothing intrinsically wrong with fast food, and the odd hamburger does no harm, if fast food constitutes a significant fraction of overall diet, as it can do, particularly in lower socio-economic groups, then you have an unbalanced, unhealthy diet.

We live in a consumerist, individualistic and materialistic society which, combined with the confusing nutritional advice, encourages the processed food industry, whose primary mission is to make money, to successfully market many 'dodgy' convenience foods and to sell them under a 'healthy eating' flag. For example, since the 1960s, nutritionists have demonised fat in food, prompting the food industry to develop countless 'low-fat' products that consumers believe are 'healthy' and non-fattening. But much of taste in food is fat based and reducing the fat content can produce a bland product. Because food must tempt the taste buds, food manufacturers often compensate for reduced fat by adding tasty high-calorie carbohydrates and the resulting 'low-fat' product may well be higher in calories than the original food with its full natural fat content. Such trickery can reach comical proportions. I recently bought hard-boiled glucose sweets in a bag bearing the prominent logo 'fat free'.

The Redeeming Power of Aerobic Exercise

Obesity statistics are compiled using a metric called the 'body mass index' (BMI) – the ratio of your weight in kilos to the square of your height in metres. A BMI below 18.5 is classed as underweight; 18.5–24.9 as normal; 25–29.9 as overweight; 30–34.9 as obese 1; 35–39.9 as obese 2; and over 40 as obese 3. You will be relieved to hear that my BMI is 24.9!

The population obesity statistics, quoted earlier, may be somewhat less depressing than they seem at first sight. Despite its widespread statistical use, BMI doesn't seem to be tightly coupled with other indicators of good health. A large study by Tomiyama, Hunger, Nguyen-Cuu, and Wells measured BMIs and metabolic health – blood pressure, blood fats, cholesterol levels, blood glucose, insulin resistance (2016). Almost 50% of BMI-classified overweight subjects, 29% of obese 1 subjects, and 16% of obese 2/3 subjects were metabolically healthy. And over 30% of BMI-classified normal weight people were metabolically unhealthy.

Waist-to-hip circumference ratio is a better index of the relationship between weight and health. A ratio over 0.9 for men and 0.85 for women indicates that abdominal obesity is a health risk.

The 2016 study results offer hope because regular aerobic exercise improves metabolic health even if you are overweight. While normal weight is undoubtedly the goal to be aimed for, prospects of enjoying good health at any body weight are significantly improved if you are aerobically fit and you eat a healthy diet. Fat but fit beats lean but unfit.

Many people are put off aerobic exercise because they think that regular vigorous walking or jogging is very hard work. But it is actually easy to establish a regular walking/running habit because the activity is so pleasurable it draws you back day after day. As you run your body releases natural opiates called endorphins that induce mild feelings of elation – 'runner's high'. If you walk or run with a companion you will find that your exercise outing is the highlight of your day.

Exercise may well be the single simple key that unlocks the conundrum of how to persuade people to adopt a healthy lifestyle. Once you become addicted to aerobic exercise your health will improve regardless of body weight and you will feel very good, both physically and mentally. You will also become more health conscious and feel more motivated to get rid of the 'jelly belly', assisted by the reduced appetite induced by the aerobic exercise.

Diet and a Sustainable Environment

Land devoted to agriculture occupies almost 40% of global landmass, the largest terrestrial ecosystem on the planet. Food production globally contributes 24% of warming greenhouse gas emissions and accounts for 70% of freshwater use. Agriculture is also a main driver of biodiversity loss.

In early 2019, *The Lancet* medical journal published a major EAT-*Lancet* Commission Report on healthy diets from sustainable food systems (Willett, Rockström, Loken et al., 2019) This report details a plant-based diet from sustainable food systems that is healthy for both people and planet and urges that it be adopted globally.

The report points out that certain foods, such as red meat, have particularly high environmental footprints and that we should eat them only in small amounts – no more than 98 grams of red meat, 203 grams of poultry and 196 grams of fish per week.

The EAT-*Lancet* Commission Report recommendations on diet are very similar to Pollan's formula, if a bit more restrictive on the amount of meat allowed. But Pollan's mantra retains the enormous advantage of being simple, short and memorable. And we must also remember that meat is a very powerful nutrient, containing all the essential amino acids your body needs, rich in B vitamins, particularly vitamin B12, and in iron and zinc. A vegan diet must have vitamin B12 supplements added.

What Should Be Done Now?

If I were Minister for Health I would take the following actions:

1. Launch a national public health campaign to publicise the simple formula for a healthy diet and lifestyle – 'Eat food, not too much, mostly plants, and take plenty of aerobic exercise.'

2. Embed this advice on diet and exercise in the education curriculum and fund healthy lifestyle activities in schools.

3. Emphasise how easily this plan can be incorporated into individual lifestyles and the guaranteed health benefits and environmental benefits that will accrue.

4. Make funds available to support public aerobic clubs (walking, jogging, cycling, swimming) countrywide.

5. Make a public declaration of trust in the Irish people to have the common sense and decency to adopt this healthy lifestyle plan.

6. Impose a reasonable tax on processed foods and soft drinks to help to fund this public health campaign.

William Reville is an emeritus of biochemistry at University College Cork.

References

Pollan, M. (2008). *In Defense of Food: An Eater's Manifesto*. New York: Penguin.

Pontzer, H. (2019, January). 'Humans Evolved to Exercise'. *Scientific American*. Available at: https://www.scientificamerican.com/article/humans-evolved-toexercise

Tomiyama, A.J., Hunger, J.M., Nguyen-Cuu, J., & Wells, C. (2016). 'Misclassification of Cardiometabolic Health when using Body Mass Index Categories in NHANES 2005–2012'. *International Journal of Obesity*, 40(5), 883.

Willett, W., Rockström, J., Loken, B., Springmann, M., Lang, T., Vermeulen, S., ... & Jonell, M. (2019). 'Food in the Anthropocene: The EAT-Lancet Commission on Healthy Diets from Sustainable Food Systems'. *The Lancet*, 393(10170), 447–492. Available at: *https://doi.org/10.1016/S0140-6736(18)31788-4*

SECTION THREE

ADDICTION

But even in the much-publicised rebellion of the young against the materialism of the affluent society, the consumer mentality is too often still intact: the standards of behaviour are still those of kind and quantity, the security sought is still the security of numbers, and the chief motive is still the consumer's anxiety that he is missing out on what is 'in'. In this state of total consumerism – which is to say a state of helpless dependence on things and services and ideas and motives that we have forgotten how to provide ourselves – all meaningful contact between ourselves and the earth is broken. We do not understand the earth in terms either of what it offers us or of what it requires of us, and I think it is the rule that people inevitably destroy what they do not understand.

Wendell Berry, *The Art of the Commonplace: The Agrarian Essays*

ADDICTION

COLIN O'GARA

An increase in population stress is reported in multiple studies from many locations worldwide. Within our addition services, I frequently observe the stress that people in Ireland are experiencing. Young couples struggle to meet high work demands and raise children, often with little support. Sleep disturbance is frequently the first noticeable effect of increased stress on the individual. This disturbance can be time-limited but occasionally progresses to a sleep disorder characterised by daytime fatigue and poor work performance. Anxiety disorders may also be a consequence of persistent stress. The anxiety may be persistent throughout the day in the form of a generalised anxiety disorder or may occur in episodic bursts of panic. Many individuals have had no access to stress management advice or training and an unexpected period of insomnia, anxiety or low mood can be very distressing. Alcohol, addictive substances and process addictions (gambling, internet gaming, pornography and excessive exercising) can provide immediate relief from these symptoms. The range of substances used to alleviate the stresses and strains of our modern society is vast at present. The most commonly used and most readily available is alcohol.

In recent years, alcohol has become more readily available in Ireland through its increased presence in off-licences, local shops and garages. Advertising has also become very frequent and sophisticated, with alcohol companies seeking to promote their products in many spheres of Irish life, particularly sporting events. The effects on our consumption of alcohol are clearly evident. Our teenagers have one of the highest rates of binge drinking in Europe. Liver disease is also a new concern for young drinkers, particularly women. It is hardly surprising, as the phrase 'wine o'clock' has become synonymous with the routine consumption of wine in the evening after a day's work or when children are in bed. Alcohol does not aid reduction in stress and insomnia, as it does not address the underlying issues leading to stress. Alcohol actually aggravates the situation as it is a substance that is very good at causing anxiety and depression. Problematic alcohol intake has effects well beyond the individual with children in particular suffering from poor parenting or various forms of abuse and neglect. Myriad alcohol related problems also present via the criminal justice system through public order offences, assault, rape and murder. The burden on our health system is substantial, with one thousand five hundred beds daily occupied by individuals with alcohol related problems.

Benzodiazepines and z-drugs are medications used in the treatment of stress, anxiety and sleep difficulties. These drugs are generally recommended for short-term use (up to two weeks for insomnia and up to four weeks for anxiety problems) and when used in the right circumstances at the correct dose can be very effective treatments. When used incorrectly, either for too long or at an incorrect dose, addiction can occur. Various estimates from the United Kingdom suggest that up to one million people are addicted to benzodiazepines. Data on the prevalence of problem benzodiazepine intake in Ireland is sparse but the problem is likely to be substantial, as it is in the United Kingdom. The rapid pace of internet development has had a major impact on how individuals access benzodiazepines. In the past, illicit sources of benzodiazepines were usually traded on the street. Nowadays the internet has allowed individuals to purchase unlimited amounts of benzodiazepines from the comfort of their front room, without any interaction whatsoever with street drug dealers. When a package of drugs arrives to the individual's home, the drug is usually consumed in an unmonitored and chaotic fashion. Much higher doses of the medication are generally purchased than would be prescribed by a doctor, with most reports of benzodiazepines available online being

'Xanax bars' which equate to two milligrams. This is a relatively strong dose of this medication and individuals can take anywhere up to twenty tablets or more in one day. An additional concern with the purchase of benzodiazepines over the internet is that individuals have no way of confirming the dose or constituents of the medication on offer. It is now commonplace for Irish drug users to have accessed all drugs they have ever taken from the internet, without ever having had contact with a drug dealer in person. Irish drug users can pay a supplement on their online drug order to have the drugs concealed in a specialised package system, unlikely to be apprehended by customs.

Prescription medications, in particular opioids, are also providing many with temporary relief from the demands of modern living. In the United States, there is an estimated one hundred and thirty deaths a day as a result of opioid overdoses. Pharmaceutical companies initially reported that these medications were not addictive but it quickly became apparent that this was not the case. The problem escalated to the extent that a state of emergency was declared in the United States in 2017. Codeine, a supposed 'weak' opioid in particular, has seen a rise in popularity in Ireland whereby individuals are consuming increasing amounts throughout the day to cope with onerous work schedules. We hear regular reports of over the counter codeine medication being taken in a widespread fashion in some workplaces. The medication is often initially taken to aid a hangover with a slow progression to taking it at several times throughout the day. It is not unusual for individuals to be taking up to seventy-two tablets in one day (three packets of twenty -four tablets). The problem of codeine addiction was acknowledged with restrictions on sale of codeine within pharmacies in Ireland in 2012. The internet has again proven to be a critical factor in the development of the problem. Reports from the United Kingdom and United States highlight the ease with which the drug is sold through online pharmacies. More concerning is the sale of prescription-only drugs like morphine, oxycodone and fentanyl. A big concern for Ireland is that the availability and rates of addiction to these powerful opioid drugs will increase to levels seen in the United States.

Irish people's current relationship with stimulants is a significant concern also. For those exhausted by the demands of modern living, cocaine can present as the perfect elixir. Prior to problems setting in with cocaine, users are transformed from lethargic, unmotivated and dysphoric to highly energised with intense focus. In the absence of accurate national prevalence data, one has to look towards the reports and trends from frontline clinical services for an indication of current usage. Within these services the reports are alarming. Cocaine is now reported to be at epidemic levels and readily available in pubs and clubs across the country. Before Ireland's economic crash in 2008, the level of cocaine consumption was a major concern. Levels of cocaine availability are now thought to be in excess of these previous boom-time highs. Patients attending our service for the treatment of cocaine addiction tell us that it is as easy to order cocaine now as it is to order a pizza. Many users also tell us that cocaine enabled them to keep going with a hectic lifestyle prior to them losing control over the drug. The problem is not restricted to young individuals either, with many seeking treatment in the over-fifty age group.

The rise of so called 'designer drugs' internationally has also brought Ireland's use of stimulants into focus. A study at Cambridge University indicated that 10% of students used a drug initially designed to treat the sleep disorder narcolepsy to enhance study performance. US data suggest that up to 20% of students have purchased concentration-enhancing drugs like modafinil which is used in the treatment of depression and/or methylphenidate, a stimulant used in the treatment of attention deficit hyperactivity disorder (ADHD) to help with their study performance. Irish student bodies have raised their concerns about the prevalence of these drugs on Irish campuses. They have highlighted the pressure students are under to pass their exams, often being subsidised by parents who are themselves under pressure to make ends meet. All drugs have potential side effects and these drugs are no different. In some cases, taking these concentration-enhancing drugs in healthy subjects has the opposite effect, leading to tiredness, lack of motivation, feelings of nausea, confusion and even psychosis.

Irish men in particular have turned to online gambling during stressful times. For some men, it promises to change their living circumstances, for others, it provides a highly accessible means of escape. Women use online gambling as a means of regulating emotions and to avoid dealing with negative emotional states. Online gambling has seen dramatic increases in usage and gambling companies are in the process of transferring the bulk of their business to the online arena. Online gambling is very accessible and provides access on a twenty-four-hour basis. Sporting events are only one aspect of the gambling product. Gamblers are also able to gamble on a full suite of casino products and 'virtual' sports events (computer generated horse or dog racing).

Video gaming has also changed dramatically because of advances in internet technology. The internet has enabled tens of thousands of video gamers to play together in games known as Massively Multiplayer Online Role-Playing Games (MMORPGs). We are currently experiencing the first wave of referrals for addiction to internet gaming. Players are losing control over the time spent engaging with these games with many reports of eight hours a day or longer. Internationally, the problem is substantial, particularly in South Korea and Japan where reports of addiction suggest up to 20% of teenagers are affected. Very high quality broadband and advances in gaming technology have contributed to the addictiveness of gaming. The increasing pressure students are under must also be a contributor.

Pornography has also become highly accessible with chatrooms and web-cams facilitating secretive, destructive sexual behaviour, often in the home, unbeknown to family members. Very often the individual reports that they lost control with pornography because of excessive stress and lifestyle imbalance.

The internet has also fuelled the rise in body image problems. Images of perfection presented on social media platforms, in particular Instagram, portray a requirement to be body perfect. This is fuelling addiction to anabolic steroids, supplements and dieting. Exercise provides many health benefits and is also highly rewarding, however, some are unable to control this rewarding effect of exercise and lose control over it. Injury follows but the individual can persist with the behaviour (exercise) in the face of these adverse consequences. Bodybuilding and extreme endurance events have risen in popularity. Both marathon and ironman events show constant ongoing yearly growth.

What Can We Do?

There is a clear need for new, well-funded public health initiatives to address the increases in alcohol, drug and process addiction difficulties. We need to acknowledge that, for many, stress presents a major life challenge and can lead to serious mental and physical health problems. Stress management programmes and workplace stress awareness training should only be part of the solution. Organisations also need to own up to the culture of workaholism and addiction when it exists within their individuals and teams. In some organisations, overworking is seen as a rite of passage in younger recruits before graduating onto higher ranks. Organisations also need to acknowledge that in permitting a culture of overworking they are facilitating the development of many of the addictive behaviours outlined above.

At a societal level, there are a number of 'quick wins' with regard to improving lifestyle and the impact of stress. Awareness campaigns highlighting the dangers of alcohol, drugs and process addictions are inadequate or non-existent at present. Restrictions in advertising of alcohol, over the counter medication and gambling is likely to yield positive results. The most obvious example is with gambling advertising where adverts are known not only to normalise gambling but also to encourage the initiation of gambling. Current gambling advertising in Ireland is not only excessive but also occurs during the day, unacceptably exposing children to potential harm.

Colin O'Gara is a consultant psychiatrist and head of addiction services in Saint John of God Hospital, Dublin.

MODERN CULTURE AND ADDICTION

JOE BARRY

From time immemorial, we human beings have had a compulsion to take psychoactive substances in order to alter our mood. What has not been there since time immemorial is the global market in most goods. Historically, people identified locally what substances occurring in nature altered the mind. In the days before mass transportation of people and goods people had a limited range of substances with which to experiment and use. In addition, mass advertising, marketing and product placement did not exist. Most substances used were cultivated and consumed locally. Subsequently, the disciplines of chemistry and pharmacology developed, which aided the manufacture and categorisation of psychoactive substances. A more modern phenomenon that has impacted very much on addiction is marketing. This applies more so in Ireland than anywhere else, as alcohol is so ingrained in our culture. Marketing and advertising developed to a very sophisticated level and Ireland has represented low-hanging fruit to the large multinational alcohol companies. In the latter half of the twentieth century, methods of mass communication advanced and the world began to shrink.

Finally, and critically, the market in illicit psychoactive drugs has also had an impact on human behaviour. Where you have a market, you have money, lots of it, and it is in this context that people are now consuming psychoactive substances. There are many ways of looking at psychoactive substances in modern Ireland.

Legal Status

There are few spaces as contested as the legal status of drugs. In Ireland, most people see illicit drugs such as heroin and cocaine in very negative terms. They are against the law, taken by people outside the mainstream, are extremely damaging to health and social functioning and are seen as a criminal justice issue. The Government in 2018 established a group to examine the potential for decriminalising certain substances. This was on foot of the publication of the latest National Drugs Strategy – *Reducing Harm, Supporting Recovery* – published in 2017 and set to run until 2025 (Department of Health, 2017). The related issue of legalisation is not being discussed and the deliberations of the group are awaited. The public perception of our most common illegal drug, cannabis, is different. Many see it as harmless, others see it as a gateway drug; some see it as a legitimate medicine for a number of clinical conditions. Speak to those who work in addiction and drug services and you will be told that street tablets, tablets bought over the internet and commonly prescribed anti-anxiety drugs are the most difficult to manage. By a very long way, our most commonly consumed drug is alcohol. It is legal and regulated but such are the norms around alcohol in Ireland that it causes a lot more harm in population terms than illegal drugs. The bottom line is that the relationship between whether a substance is legal and the harm that it causes is not what most people think.

Social Profile

Opiates are overwhelmingly used by people from deprived backgrounds and this social connection is more important than biological or even psychological factors. If one wants to improve matters in relation to opiates in Ireland, the most important area on which to focus in the biopsychosocial model is the social one. Open dealing of drugs is tolerated in parts of Ireland, Dublin in particular, that would not be tolerated in other countries. Most citizens never brush up against this, even though it happens a few metres from O'Connell Street, the main thoroughfare of our capital city. Gangland shootings, often related to the illicit drugs trade, are common, and brutal violence is meted out to people on a regular basis. The way stimulant drug use is reported in Ireland mirrors this social approach to opiates. Celebrities who use cocaine, and sometimes unfortunately die as a result, command much media attention. Poor people using cocaine or crack cocaine get little mention. One Irish person dies from a drug overdose every day.

The only category of drug taken by women more than men is prescribed medication. These drugs are marketed to doctors by the pharmaceutical industry. Once the drug is sold the pharmaceutical company has its money made. These drugs are now commodities on our streets, traded between different sectors of society. The number of deaths from these medications is rising in Ireland.

Alcohol is ubiquitous in Ireland. While we have the highest percentage of teetotallers in the EU, we also have very high rates of heavy and harmful drinking; heavy episodic drinking, colloquially known as binge drinking. Unlike heavy and harmful cigarette smoking, which occurs mostly among poorer people, harmful drinking is common in higher income groups. An illustration of this comes from a Royal College of Physicians of Ireland study which showed that, while Irish hospital doctors are much less likely to smoke cigarettes than the general population, they are much more likely to be alcohol drinkers. Alcohol is seen by many as a stress reliever; get home from work in the evening, kick off your shoes and have a beer (men) or wine (women). A manifestation of the grip alcohol has on our national psyche is the fact that Ireland is probably the only country in the world where people opting not to drink alcohol at an event will get quizzed as to why. Another is the pressure teenagers who do not drink can come under from their peers. These social norms and subtle influences on our national psyche are carefully and subliminally promoted and nurtured by the alcohol industry, who, until recently, faced little opposition to their preferred narrative. Attitudes to changing this culture are mixed; women are more in favour of change than men. A very apparent illustration of this phenomenon is the very strong association between rugby and alcohol, to the extent that the rugby authorities in Ireland have stated, during their long and ongoing opposition to the ending of sports sponsorship by alcohol companies, that the game has become dependent on alcohol sponsorship. Another manifestation is the sustained opposition to the passage of the Public Health (Alcohol) Bill by the Oireachtas (over one thousand days); this opposition was more sustained in Seanad Éireann. Opposition to the commencement of the various elements of the new act will be next. Separately, a campaign to reverse changes to life-saving drink driving legislation has begun, with high profile political support. This originated with vintners and will be presented as another front in the fight to save rural Ireland.

Harms

Why does all this matter? It matters because of the immense harms to the fabric of our society brought about by the sophisticated (alcohol companies) and brutal (criminal gangs) methods employed by those who are profiting from the use of these products. Each group is driven by profit and the damage inflicted does not seem to matter – prolonged hospital visits; half of all suicides; a large percentage of accidental deaths from drowning, in house fires and on our roads (less now because of legislation, though this is being challenged); crowded courts; shootings; deaths from blood- borne viruses; and intimidation of whole communities.

What Can Be Done?

All communities are entitled to the same level of protection from drug dealing; nobody will deny that, but it is not the reality. That may be a matter of resources but it is also a matter of political priorities. People who use opiates are overrepresented in the homeless population (median age at death in Dublin of forty years) and in our prisons. Life is short if you are homeless and not pleasant. Our government says there is enough money to deal with the homeless problem; they must have very modest ambitions for their fellow citizens without a home. Modern Irish governments do not build houses the way their predecessors did.

Young people must remain within the school system until the age of sixteen, preferably eighteen. There is strong evidence that drug dealers can spot vulnerable children and groom them from a very early age, in the same way that sexual predators do. Modern Ireland's education system does not invest in initiatives aimed at retaining vulnerable children in school.

One of the best legacies parents in Ireland can pass to their children is to delay the onset of alcohol consumption. The evidence tells us that children who begin drinking in their teens have a four-fold increase in dependence in later life. Ireland can be a tough place for children aged between fourteen and seventeen who do not want to drink alcohol. Marketing is relentless, sports sponsorship by alcohol companies is lauded and school-based alcohol education is dwarfed by the marketing and advertising budgets of the alcohol companies. On a practical note, introducing your child to alcohol in the home is not recommended as a strategy to lessen the chances that your child will have problems with alcohol. Well-off families and families in the east of the country are much more likely to think this is a good strategy than poorer families and those in more rural parts of the country.

Other Addictions

Outside of psychotropic addictions, the next most prominent and rising addiction in the public's awareness is gambling addiction. Gambling addiction is not generally addressed in mainstream addiction services, which focus on psychotropics. There are anecdotal reports that gambling companies block the accounts of people who win money from them and facilitate people who lose a lot to keep on gambling. Moves to improve matters by legislation are resisted by the gambling industry. In the same way that the organisation known as Drinkaware is funded by the alcohol industry with the aim of preventing the passage and implementation of effective legislation that would limit the reach of alcohol in society, so also the gambling industry has established the organisation Betaware. There is a global pattern where industries that account for large numbers of addicted persons (such as the alcohol, tobacco or gambling industries) lobby very hard, and with vast sums of money at their disposal, in order to prevent effective measures getting on the statute books of various countries; Ireland is no different in this regard.

The industries that have established and promoted the mass distribution of substances or activities prone to dependence have succeeded because power is now concentrated in a relatively small number of mega corporations around the world and they bring resources and financial backing that is larger than the economic outputs of whole countries. These companies relentlessly chase profits and new markets across the globe. If one country develops strong regulation, the companies expand to other populous countries where regulation is weak. Regulation works; imagine how the financial crash in this country might have had a less negative impact if robust regulation were in place.

Politics

Is there hope for the future? For the sake of the planet, there must be. The general populations in many countries are becoming much more critical of large multinational corporations than previously; the social media giants, the alcohol and food industries and the fossil fuel promoters to name just a few. People are asking: Who rules the world? Is it big corporations, or governments? It is through ordinary citizens mobilising their efforts and joining civic society groups that change will happen. School children are now showing the way to governments. Winston Churchill said that democracy was the least worst form of government. Our multi-seat constituency model accentuates clientelist politics at the expense of the common good. It turns politicians into followers rather than leaders and even the politicians most committed to change in Ireland have to play the local clientelist game to get re-elected. Those best at the clientelist game often top the poll and they are generally hostile to regulation; be it climate change denial that will destroy the planet, alcohol policy that will exacerbate our health and social problems or local planning issues that will ruin the environment.

Joe Barry is professor of population health medicine, Trinity College, Dublin. Research interests include: a programmatic and thematic approach to research into problem substance use and addiction.

Reference

Department of Health. (2017). *Reducing Harm, Supporting Recovery: A Health-led Response to Drug and Alcohol Use in Ireland 2017–2025.*

SECTION FOUR

SUSTAINABILITY

> We can't just consume our way to a more sustainable world.
>
> **Jennifer Nini**

CLIMATE CHANGE

JOHN GIBBONS

On the eve of the third decade of the twenty-first century, awareness among the Irish public of climate change being probably the defining issue of our times has gone from the fringes to the mainstream.

The global 'school strike for climate', which took place in March 2019, saw thousands of young people from all over the country pour onto the streets to demand that Ireland do its fair share in tackling the crisis. In Dublin alone, an estimated fifteen thousand young people filled the streets around Leinster House in a good-humoured but entirely serious show of force.

The message from the streets was clear: today's political leadership has been 'asleep at the wheel' as the climate crisis grew, in real time, from scientific theory to ever more ineffable evidence of the biosphere teetering on the edge of collapse.

The rapid evisceration of the natural world is happening at a pace that almost defies description. In just the five decades since 1970, around two-thirds of all wild land animals have disappeared. Since the 1950s, the world's oceans have become 30% more acidic, and global population of sea birds has declined by around 70%.

In the same period, levels of atmospheric carbon dioxide (CO_2), the trace 'greenhouse gas', have increased by nearly 40%, to their highest levels in at least three million years. In Europe and elsewhere, widespread and rapid collapses in insect populations have been recorded. Since 1991, total recorded flying insect populations in Germany have fallen by an astonishing 78%.

The UN Environment Programme (UNEP) describes it in these terms: 'The world is currently undergoing a very rapid loss of biodiversity comparable with the great mass extinction events that have previously occurred only five times in the Earth's history' (World Wildlife Fund, 2002). To take just one example, every year, the felling of forests is depriving the world of some $2.5 *trillion* of critical environmental services. The UNEP estimates that some 60% of the Earth's natural resources have been 'severely degraded' in just the last quarter century.

None of the facts outlined in the foregoing paragraphs are either controversial or particularly obscure. The scientific evidence pointing to dangerous overshoot of human activities and impacts on the natural world is abundant and, at least within the halls of science, beyond any dispute.

The Intergovernmental Panel on Climate Change (IPCC) has, over the last three decades, been the largest interdisciplinary global scientific collaboration the world has ever seen. In this period, it has produced five full-scale Assessment Reports and numerous specialist reports, bringing together and distilling the findings from tens of thousands of scientists working across dozens of specialties.

The sheer scale of this mammoth task, combined with the need to achieve political sign-off from world governments on the final document, means that IPCC reports have always tended to err on the side of conservatism rather than alarmism.

Notwithstanding this, the IPCC's Fifth Assessment Report, issued in November 2014 included the following chillingly unambiguous warning: 'Human influence on the climate system is clear and growing, with impacts observed on all continents. If left unchecked, climate change will increase the likelihood of *severe, pervasive and irreversible impacts* for people and ecosystems' (IPCC, 2014; emphasis added).

In December of the following year, the UN conference met in the French capital and, after two weeks of negotiations, the Paris Agreement was issued, and some one hundred and ninety-seven countries (including Ireland, as an EU member) signed this legally binding agreement. The Paris Agreement sets out a medium-term goal to put the world on track to limit global warming to well below 2°C centigrade above pre-industrial levels and to 'pursue efforts' to limit the temperature increase to 1.5°C.

Considering that average global temperatures are already slightly more than 1°C above pre-industrial, the scope to avoid breaching the 1.5°C guard rail seems slight. In fact, in the unlikely event that every country on Earth actually achieved 100% of its commitments under the Paris Agreement, global temperatures are still expected to rise by a deadly 3.3°C by 2100. And some major polluters, notably Russia, Iran and the US, have all but renounced their Paris targets.

Ireland is a small country, with a small population, yet we exert an oversized 'carbon footprint'. We emit around sixty million tonnes of greenhouse gases annually, which averages at around thirteen tonnes per person. Since 1990, Ireland's emissions per person have risen by just under 50%.

In the same period, Sweden, a country with at least as high a standard of living as Ireland, has reduced its emissions per person by 15%. The average Swede today accounts for less than half the carbon emissions of their Irish counterpart. In fact, Irish emissions are today 45% higher than the EU average.

The Irish government signed up at EU level to reduce our emissions by 2020 by a total of 20% versus 2005. With this deadline almost upon us, we will achieve, 'at best', an overall reduction of around 1%, according to figures from the Environment Protection Agency (EPA, 2018). This means Ireland will be facing annual non-compliance fines of an estimated €500–€600 million per annum throughout the 2020s.

With the highest average wind speeds in western Europe, Ireland would be expected to be a leader in renewable energy. The opposite is the case. Some 88% of our total energy comes from imported sources, compared to an EU average of around 50%. Apart from importing over €6 billion in fossil fuels annually, Ireland also burns domestic peat in three power stations.

Data from the Central Statistics Office (CSO, 2016a) shows the Irish government provided €115 million in subsidies for peat-fired electricity in 2016. In the same year, just €88 million was made available in subsidies to retrofit homes for energy efficiency. The massive peat subsidy is levied on all electricity users via the so-called Public Service Obligation (PSO) charged directly onto users' bills.

While peat power provides just 9% of our electricity, it generates around 23% of total energy sector emissions. Peat bog mining also involves the complete destruction of areas of high ecological sensitivity and biodiversity. The pointless, loss-making and environmentally destructive peat mining is symptomatic of the wider failures in Irish society and politics to begin to grasp our ecological responsibilities.

Emissions from Ireland's transport and agriculture sectors are both continuing to climb. The number of private cars on Irish roads has more than doubled since 1996, to well over two million today, leading to congestion, air pollution and soaring carbon emissions. Car dependence has also fed into increasingly sedentary lifestyles and a sharp rise in diabetes and obesity, even among the young. In 1986, just under 50% of Irish children either walked or cycled to primary school, according to CSO data (CSO, 2016). Just thirty years later, this had fallen to below 25% by 2016.

There has been an upswing in people cycling to work, with numbers rising by 43% since 2011, albeit from a low base. Despite this, attitudes to cycling at political, local authority and law enforcement level remain ambiguous at best, and often openly hostile. The very politicians who laud the opening of a 'green way' cycle path often seem unable to imagine cycling as a serious option for daily commuting.

Heavily influenced by industry lobbyists, Irish government policy on transport has been to double down on road and motorway building. For instance, funding of over €600 million was recently approved for a bypass for part of Galway city. The degree to which this is overtly or covertly influenced by a media heavily dependent on motor industry advertising and sponsorship is only recently being seriously explored.

Sustainable transport initiatives, for instance the development of protected cycle lanes, receives only a tiny single-digit percentage of the capital expenditure that locks in carbon air pollution-intensive modes of transport.

This lack of political commitment to following the successful European model of heavy investment into high-quality, high-frequency and low-cost public transport, allied with enhanced safe spaces for walking and cycling, has forced many people into the trap of car dependence.

This in turn leads to more congestion, longer commutes, poorer health and fitness levels and less disposable income, as the high running costs of private cars place a heavy toll especially on younger families.

Ireland's agriculture sector is our number one source of greenhouse gas emissions, accounting for almost one-third of total emissions. The reason our emissions in this sector are so unusual by European standards is that Ireland is heavily weighted towards dairy and beef production, the two most emissions-intensive forms of agriculture.

Despite massive investment by Bord Bia, the Irish Food Board in the 'Origin Green' programme attempting to capitalise on Ireland's 'green' image to promote our model of food production as being both 'natural' and 'sustainable', the data suggests it is in fact neither.

A 2017 report issued by the European Commission found that, when the amount of carbon emissions per euro of agricultural output was measured, Ireland had the worst ratio in the entire EU28 (EP, 2017).

This study's findings were backed up in 2019 with the publication by the UN Food & Agriculture Organisation (UN-FAO) of its Global Livestock Environmental Assessment Model (GLEAM) data. Its methodology is to examine the full life/cycle impact of food production. It found that Ireland is the most carbon-intensive beef producer in Europe, and ranks as Europe's third highest on emissions from its dairy sector.

Significant efforts have been made by politicians in arguing that Ireland should be allowed to continue to expand its dairy sector in particular, on the grounds that our largely grass-fed model is both efficient and sustainable. The evidence above suggests it is in fact neither.

Also, according to the Environmental Protection Agency (EPA), there has been a notable decline in Irish water quality. Some two hundred and sixty-nine Irish waterways, which include rivers, coastal areas, canals, estuaries and lakes, deteriorated in quality between 2015 and 2017. The main cause of this decline is the nitrogen and phosphorus used in artificial fertilisers.

Air quality is also declining. EPA data for 2016 found that ammonia, nitrogen oxides and non-methane volatile organic compounds were, for the first time, all above recommended EU emissions levels in 2016 (EPA, 2018). In order to be able to support over seven million beef and dairy cattle, Ireland has obtained a series of derogations from the EU Nitrates Directive, which aims to protect air and water quality from excessive nitrogen usage.

The powerful agribusiness lobby has fought successfully to prevent carbon taxes being levied on high-emissions foodstuffs, as recommended by the report of the Citizens' Assembly on climate change in late 2017. It is also notable that, despite its attempt at 'green' branding, Ireland has the second lowest percentage (1.6%) of its agricultural land farmed organically in the EU, and the lowest percentage of land used for horticulture.

Ireland has spent tens of millions in major marketing efforts to portray our food industry internationally as uniquely 'green', and by extension, environmentally sustainable. Bord Bia, the state agency for promoting Irish food and drink, has invested heavily in its 'Origin Green' programme.

It has come under fire from another state agency, Teagasc, the body responsible for agricultural research and development, stating that the industry needs 'credible evidence rather than glamour stories' about sustainability. Organic farming is by far the most environmentally sustainable form of agriculture. It also offers higher prices to producers and lower input costs.

Within Europe, growing concerns over the environmental and health impacts of intensive agriculture is leading to a consumer backlash, as more people are demanding that their food be free of pesticides and herbicides. Austria, Sweden and Estonia already have close to one-fifth of all agricultural land farmed organically, compared to well below 2% in 'green' Ireland.

The market in the EU for organic foods has quadrupled in the last fifteen years, and is now valued at over €33 billion annually, a fast-growing market almost all Irish farmers are missing out on. Over 70% of all organic fruit and vegetables sold in Ireland are imported.

According to data from the Central Statistics Office, in 2017, Ireland imported a total of one hundred and eighty six thousand tonnes of potatoes, onions, tomatoes, cabbage and lettuce, with a value of €175 million (CSO, 2017). While once synonymous with Ireland, in 2017 we imported forty-four tonnes of potatoes from Britain alone, while total Irish potato exports amounted to a paltry three thousand tonnes.

Conclusion

As the foregoing sets out, Ireland is, in the Taoiseach's own words, an international 'laggard' on climate action. To date, the debate in Ireland has tended to focus on the costs of taking steps to address climate change. These narratives are promoted by well-funded lobbyists and only opposed by environmental NGOs with minimal funding and extremely limited political access.

The year 2019 may come to be seen as one in which the pendulum began to swing. Following the children's school strike, other groups, including 'Extinction Rebellion' engaged in acts of peaceful civil disobedience, continuing a long tradition of resistance. The publication in early 2019 of a strong joint Oireachtas Committee on Climate Action report signalled a shift in political attitudes and a long-overdue awakening to the existential nature of the climate crisis (Joint Committee on Climate Action, 2019).

In turn, this is gradually rippling into how the media covers environment and climate issues. Big wheels, however, turn slowly, but it is likely that fast-growing public anxiety and anger over climate inaction (as brilliantly articulated by Swedish teenager Greta Thunberg) may see the pace of response increase markedly in the early 2020s.

Whether it keeps pace with the rapid onset of widespread biodiversity collapse and climate breakdown remains to be seen.

John Gibbons is an Irish environmental campaigner and the founder of the *climatechange.ie* website.

References

Central Statistics Office. (2016). *Census of Population 2016 – Profile 6 Commuting in Ireland*. Available at: https://www.cso.ie/en/releasesandpublications/ep/p-cp6ci/p6cii/p6stp/

Central Statistics Office. (2016a). *Research Paper: Fossil Fuel and Similar Subsidies 2012–2016*. Available at: https://www.cso.ie/en/media/csoie/releasespublications/documents/rp/fossilfuelandsimilarsubsidies/Fossil_Fuel_and_Similar_Subsidies.pdf

Central Statistics Office. (2017). *Ireland's Trade in Goods 2017 – Food 2017*. Available at: https://www.cso.ie/en/releasesandpublications/ep/p-ti/irelandstradeingoods2017/food2017/

Environmental Protection Agency. (2018). *We need to move away from fossil fuels, EPA emissions projections show*. Available at: http://www.epa.ie/newsandevents/news/pressreleases2018/name,64049,en.html

European Parliament. (2017). *Research for Agri Committee – Policy Support for Productivity vs. Sustainability in EU Agriculture*. Available at: http://www.europarl.europa.eu/RegData/etudes/STUD/2017/585905/IPOL_STU(2017)585905_EN.pdf

Environmental Protection Agency. (2018). *Emissions of three important air pollutants increased in 2016 – Ireland's emissions going in the wrong direction for people to benefit from cleaner air*. Available at: https://www.epa.ie/newsandevents/news/pressreleases2018/name,63848,en.html

Intergovernmental Panel on Climate Change. (2014, 2 November). *Concluding Instalment of the Fifth Assessment Report: Climate Change Threatens Irreversible and Dangerous Impacts, but Options Exist to Limit its Effects*. Switzerland: IPCC.

Joint Committee on Climate Action. (2019). *Climate Change: A Cross-Party Consensus for Action*. Available at: https://data.oireachtas.ie/ie/oireachtas/committee/dail/32/joint_committee_on_climate_action/reports/2019/2019-03-28_report-climate-change-a-cross-party-consensus-for-action_en.pdf

World Wildlife Fund. (2002). *Living Planet Report 2002: Summary*. Switzerland: WWF International.

PATHWAYS TO SUSTAINABILITY

JOHN SWEENEY

Over the course of the last century, global average life expectancy has more than doubled, and is now nearing seventy years. Over many parts of the developed world, a child born today can expect to live for over eighty years. This represents an astonishing turnaround in longevity. A century ago life expectancy in India and South Korea was around twenty-three years, and it was as late as the 1950s before it rose above thirty-six years in Africa (Roser, 2019). Improved health care, better nutrition, housing and education, have all played a central role in this. But the paradox is that this radical improvement in the human condition has occurred as global environmental degradation has plumbed new depths. A spectrum of environmental drivers, headed by climate change, but including air and water pollution, freshwater scarcity, land and ocean degradation and major losses of biodiversity, now threatens the very existence of humankind in anything like contemporary numbers in the long, and possibly medium, term. The realisation that our present well-being is achieved by mortgaging the options for future generations is now a stark reality, part of the defining characteristics of what has now become known as the Anthropocene Epoch.

Although the birth of awareness of the human impact on the life support systems of the planet is rightly credited to Rachel Carson and her pioneering text *Silent Spring* published in the early 1960s, it was later that the interconnections between population growth, economics and resource exploitation began to be quantitatively explored. The emergence of computing simulations in the 1970s, by groups such as the Club of Rome (Meadows, Randers & Behrens III, 1972), brought to public prominence the fact that living on a finite planet meant that there were ultimately limits to growth. Although widely criticised for its mechanistic approach and simplifying assumptions, there was an underlying logic to *Limits to Growth* which could not be denied and indeed has resurfaced in the form of the concept of planetary boundaries.

The most recent expression of this is provided by Kate Raworth (2017). Figure 1 shows nine planetary boundaries, an ecological ceiling beyond which major environmental degradation and potential tipping points in Earth systems are likely to occur. The twelve components of the social foundation are based on standards underpinning the UN Sustainable Development Goals agreed in 2015. Between the social and planetary boundaries, an environmentally safe and socially just space exists. This is where humanity must operate and where its life support systems are sustainable.

The intrinsic simplicity of such an approach is the manner in which it integrates social, economic and environmental considerations. The dominance of the economic paradigm is challenged. The concept of tipping points becomes an ingredient to consider regarding growth. Social justice underpins economics and environmental considerations. Pathways to sustainability are hinted at but no particular political ideology is advocated.

Four of the nine planetary boundaries were reported as having been crossed by 2015: climate change, loss of biosphere integrity, land-system change, and altered biogeochemical cycles (phosphorus and nitrogen) (Steffen et al., 2015). It might be thought that these events come about as a result of a gradual assault on the environmental systems of the planet, and that by rectifying them a restoration of the status quo can be achieved. This is mistaken. It is now appreciated that the planet will accommodate itself to new circumstances via step changes in its functioning. These may or may not be more favourable to individual components such as the human ecosystem. Sensitivity to such 'tipping points' is particularly well exemplified by climate change. For long the concept of 'dangerous climate change' was not quantified, and the concept was at risk of becoming a cliché. Schneider and Lane (2006) suggested more concrete measurement criteria, many of which were based around tipping points:

- Risks to unique and threatened geophysical or biophysical systems
- Risks associated with extreme weather events
- Total damages
- Temperature thresholds to large-scale events
- Risks to global and local ecosystems
- Loss of human cultures
- 'Millions at risk' – the additional number of millions of people placed at risk
- The five key sustainability metrics: water, energy, health, agriculture, and biodiversity
- Impacts at a pace beyond the capacity to adapt
- Triggering of an irreversible chain of events
- Early warning dangers present in certain areas that are likely to spread and worsen over time with increased warming
- Distributional metrics: inter-country equity, intergenerational equity, and inter-species equity

In the build-up to the Paris Agreement, these criteria crystallised around a more simple metric, namely that of a 2°C warming above pre-industrial levels. The wisdom of this can be seen in Figure 2 where Schellnhuber, Rahmstorf and Winkelmann (2016) have placed the 'burning embers' diagram of the Intergovernmental Panel on Climate Change Assessment Report against temperature thresholds at which commencement and final destruction of elements in the climate system are likely to occur. It is clear that serious consequences commence before the 2°C line is crossed, especially in the marine biosphere.

It is also the case that global sustainability is not accompanied by regional sustainability. In the closing stages of the Paris Conference of the Parties (COP21), it was argued by the small island developing states that 2°C warming would eliminate many of their homelands via the associated sea-level rise. For this reason, a report on the impacts of 1.5°C warming was commissioned from the IPCC. Published in late 2018, this revealed the scale of global decarbonisation necessary to avoid both temperature thresholds. Figure 3 indicates that sustainability, at least for the small island developing states, requires 45% emission reductions globally by 2030 and wider global sustainability, as defined by remaining below 2°C warming, requires zero net anthropogenic carbon dioxide emissions within the next thirty years. Of course, even on the road to attaining these difficult targets, major dislocation in terms of climate extremes, sea-level rise, and losses of biodiversity will occur.

Deeply entrenched in our psyche is the concept that growth is good, that growth is inevitable, and that growth equates to social and economic progress. The dominance of the economic paradigm to the exclusion of ethical concerns for the next generation, and even for the other lifeforms we share the planet with, is overwhelming. The dilemma for environmentalists is whether sustainability concerns should be expressed within the economic paradigm or contest it from the outside.

Monetisation of environmental variables is one such approach to reconciling environmental sustainability with economic arguments for growth-centred approaches. Valuation of environmental goods and services as part of an overall economy is the basis of this approach. What service does a peat bog, or coastal dunes, or a colony of bees provide? Can a monetary value be placed on this, for example, to be set against actions that might result in their damage or loss for profitable gain? This is not easy. Environmental goods and services frequently do not have markets and therefore are difficult to price. They may be public goods which are vulnerable to the 'Tragedy of the Commons' (Hardin, 1968) or they may not be amenable to valuation in terms of changing value systems of future generations. This makes it difficult to incorporate them into decision-making, for example, as components in an environmental impact assessment or in a cost-benefit analysis. The economic dimension is, by contrast, easily quantifiable in terms of jobs, income flows, etc. Costanza et al. (1997) valued the world's ecosystem services in the range €12–€40 trillion per annum, while at a smaller scale Bullock, Kretsch and Candon. (2008) estimated the total marginal value of ecosystem services in Ireland at €2.6 billion per annum. But the assumptions and caveats underlying such estimates are substantial and the inherent uncertainties render it unlikely that the approach will ever enter mainstream economic thinking on the scale necessary to make a difference.

Gross Domestic Product (GDP) has for a long time been used as a surrogate for the health of an economy. It is now clear that it is a flawed instrument, not least when it comes to providing an indication of social and environmental well-being. Aspects such as income distribution, non-paid work, environmental damage, social stresses from commuting and crime, etc., do not figure in this classical measure. Attempts at monetisation of these are subject to assumptions and problems. However, attempts at their incorporation can provide a better measure of social and environmental well-being, and, thus, whether a trajectory of more or less sustainability is being followed. A sophisticated index, the National Welfare Index (NWI), incorporating nineteen variables (Table 1) has been developed by German researchers (Diefenbacher, Held, Rodenhäuser & Zieschank, 2016) and is increasingly used by the German Länder to inform decision-making by integrating social and environmental concerns with conventional economic assessments. At a national scale, this exercise in monetisation of variables that are not usually incorporated provides an insight into divergences over time between GDP and the NWI (Figure 4). It can be seen that between 1991 and 1998 German GDP and NWI moved in tandem, but since then they have diverged with continuing GDP growth but the NWI essentially back to where it was in the early 1990s. In this case, increasing income inequality and increased environmental damage has been implicated as the cause of the divergence (Diefenbacher et al., 2016). Increased wealth has not been accompanied by increased well-being and sustainability.

Recognising the difficulties of working within the economic paradigm to address sustainability issues has led many to advocate on ethical, legal and moral grounds. Environmental justice, especially climate justice, frames sustainability as an ethical and political issue, informed by science, but centred on human concerns of stewardship and environmental equity. For example, a relatively small country such as Ireland emits more greenhouse gases annually than the eight hundred million poorest people on Earth. Yet the loss and damage the developing world suffers does not produce actions in the developed world to rectify this. As a result, environmental justice movements increasingly recognise the need to address powerful vested interest groups either directly through litigation or by encouraging actions such as divestment from fossil fuel investments. Both means have captured the attention of a younger generation who see themselves as future victims of unsustainable current trends. Divestment campaigns have grown rapidly in effectiveness and have now succeeded in releasing €5 trillion of funds. Litigation against governments and corporations has also become widespread. Outside the United States, some two hundred cases have been taken, while inside the US the comparable figure is over one thousand. But it is individuals who have mobilised public opinion. The Swedish schoolgirl Greta Thunberg has sensitised young people on a hitherto unimaginable scale by her school strikes actions and her direct appeal to decision makers and big business. A similar message has emanated from the highly influential second encyclical of Pope Francis, *Laudato Si'*, addressed to 'every person living on this planet', where a new paradigm of justice based on integral ecology is advocated as a means of tackling the closely related social and environmental crises the world currently faces.

In conclusion, the much-debased word 'sustainability' has not yet permeated the consciousness of most of the population of the planet, people who are concerned with day-to-day matters and who find it difficult to reconcile slow deterioration of the life support systems of the Earth with individual actions and longer-term changes in their aspirations and lifestyles. The long-standing commodification of the environment remains a deeply ingrained barrier to new thinking. Health concerns, food security and climate vulnerability will undoubtedly be catalysts in challenging these preconceptions and hopefully educating the general population to appreciate the urgency of achieving the radical changes necessary for sustainability. But the jury is still out on whether implementing these changes will occur in time to ensure the sustainability of 'Our Common Home'.

John Sweeney has been a lecturer at Maynooth University Geography Department since 1978. He currently leads a number of nationally funded research projects examining various aspects of climate change in Ireland.

References

Bullock, C., Kretsch, C., & Candon, E. (2008). *The Economic and Social Aspect of Biodiversity: Benefits and Costs of Biodiversity in Ireland.* Department of Environment, Heritage and Local Government, Dublin.

Carson, R. (1962). *Silent Spring*. Boston: Houghton Mifflin.

Costanza, R., d'Arge, R., De Groot, R., Farber, S., Grasso, M., Hannon, B., ... & Raskin, R.G. (1997). 'The value of the world's ecosystem services and natural capital'. *Nature,* 387(6630), 253–260.

Diefenbacher, H., Held, B., Rodenhäuser, D., & Zieschank, R. (2016). *Wohlfahrtsmessung 'Beyond GDP' Der Nationale Wohlfahrtsindex (NWI2016)* Hans-Böckler-Stiftung. Dusseldorf, Germany.

Hardin, G. (1968). 'The Tragedy of the Commons'. *Science*, 162(3859): 1243–1248.
IPCC. (2018). 'Summary for Policymakers'. *Global Warming of 1.5°C. An IPCC Special Report on the impacts of global warming of 1.5°C above pre-industrial levels and related global greenhouse gas emission pathways, in the context of strengthening the global response to the threat of climate change, sustainable development, and efforts to eradicate poverty* (Masson-Delmotte, V., P. Zhai, H.-O. Pörtner, D. Roberts, J. Skea, P.R. Shukla, A. Pirani, W. Moufouma-Okia, C. Péan, R. Pidcock, S. Connors, J.B.R. Matthews, Y. Chen, X. Zhou, M.I. Gomis, E. Lonnoy, T. Maycock, M. Tignor, & T. Waterfield [eds]). Geneva: World Meteorological Organization.
Meadows, D.H., Meadows, D.L., Randers, J., & Behrens III, W. (1972). *The Limits to Growth: A Report for the Club of Rome's Project on the Predicament of Mankind.* New York: Universe Books.
Raworth, K. (2017). *Doughnut Economics: Seven Ways to Think Like a 21st Century Economist*. London: Penguin Random House.
Roser. (2019). 'Life Expectancy'. Published online at *OurWorldInData.org*. Available at: https://ourworldindata.org/life-expectancy
Schellnhuber, H.J., Rahmstorf, S., Winkelmann, R. (2016). 'Why the Right Climate Target was Agreed in Paris'. *Nature Climate Change*. Available at: DOI: 10.1038/nclimate3013
Schneider, S.H., & Lane, J. (2006). 'An Overview of Dangerous Climate Change'. *Avoiding Dangerous Climate Change*, 7(11).
Steffen, W., Richardson, K., Rockström, J., Cornell, S.E., Fetzer, I., Bennett, E.M., Biggs, R., Carpenter, S.R., de Vries, W., de Wit, C.A., Folke, C., Gerten, D., Heinke, J., Mace, G.M., Persson, L.M., Ramanathan, V., Reyers, B. and Sorlin, S. (2015). 'Planetary Boundaries: Guiding Human Development on a Changing Planet'. *Science*, 347(6223). Available at: DOI: 10.1126/science.1259855

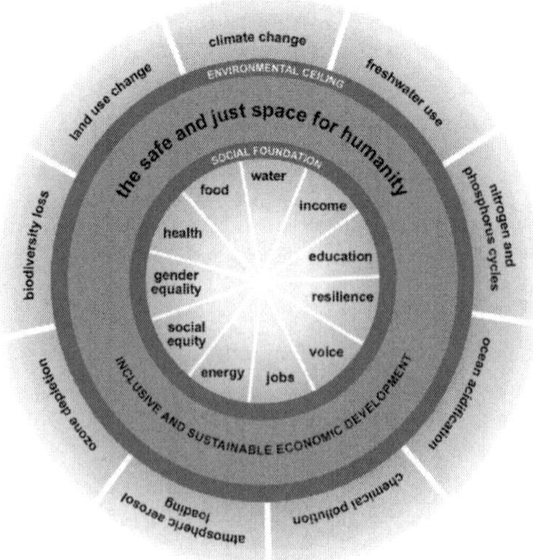

Figure 1: The Doughnut of social and planetary boundaries (Source: Raworth (2017) WAIS: West Antarctic Ice Sheet THC: Thermo-Haline Circulation ENSO: El Niño Southern Oscillation EAIS: East Antarctic Ice Sheet

Figure 2: Tipping points triggered at global temperature increases both at the Paris range (1.5-2°C) and at higher levels associated with a failure to peak global greenhouse gas emissions (RCP approximates to 2040 peaking, RCP6.0 to 2080 and RCP8.5 to continued increases in emissions beyond 2080) (Source: Schellnhuber, Rahmstorf and Winkelmann, 2016)

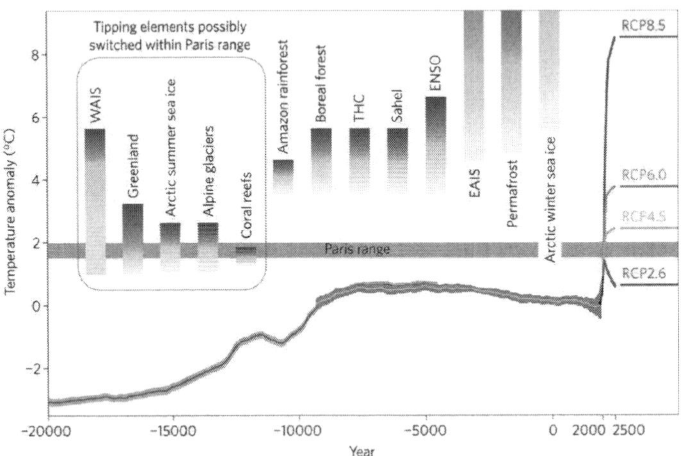

Figure 3: Mitigation pathways to avoid 1.5°C/2°C warming (After IPCC, 2018)

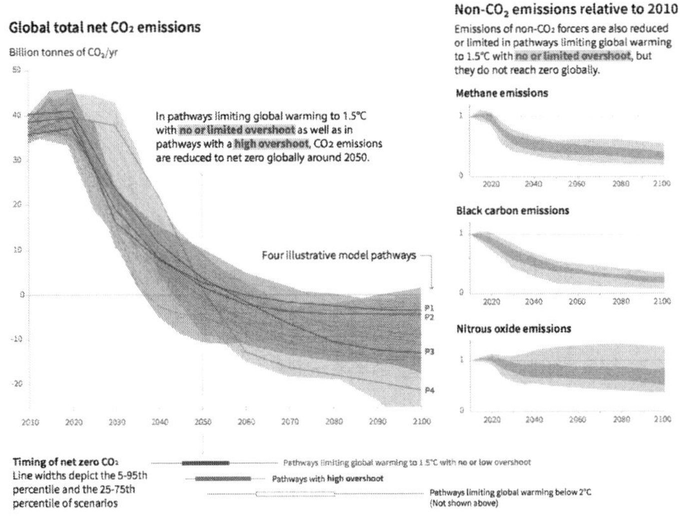

Figure 4: The National Welfare Index and GDP for Germany 1991-2016

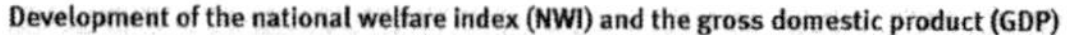

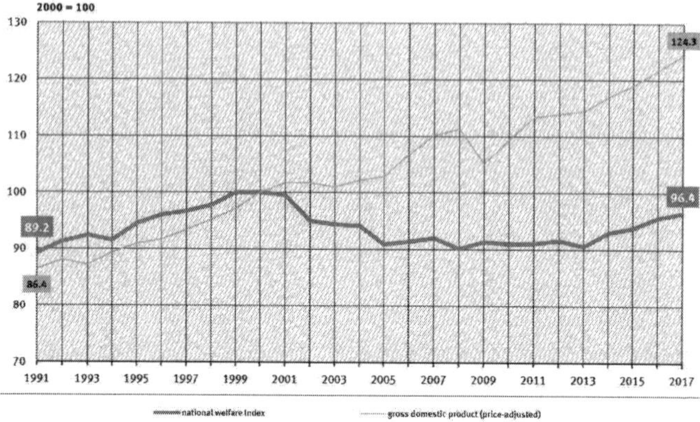

Table 1: Components of the German National Welfare Index

Index of income distribution	Weighted consumer spending	Value of domestic work	Value of voluntary work
Public spending on health/ education	Costs and benefits of consumer durable	Costs of commuting between home and work	Cost of traffic accidents
Costs of crime	Costs of alcohol, tobacco, drug use	Social costs of compensation for environmental damage	Damage due to water pollution
Damage due to impacts on soil	Effects of air pollution	Damage due to noise	Loss/gain through changes to habitat
Damage due to loss of arable land	Substitution costs generated by exploitation of non-renewable resources	Damage due to CO_2 emissions	Costs of nuclear energy use

HOW TO REDUCE AGRICULTURAL EMISSIONS?

ALAN MATTHEWS

Agriculture and the land-use sector have a key role to play in Ireland's proclaimed desire to take a leadership role in addressing the dangers of climate change. Agriculture is the single largest source of greenhouse gas (GHG) emissions in Ireland, accounting for 33% of our total national emissions (by contrast, transport accounts for 20% and energy generation for a further 20%). Of the just over twenty million tonnes of CO2e from agricultural emissions, around thirteen million tonnes CO2e are due to methane arising from the process of digestion in ruminant animals (mainly cattle and sheep) as well as the management of manure. A further six million tonnes of CO2e are due to the release of nitrous oxide following the application of manure and fertiliser to agricultural soils (note that CO2e, which stands for carbon dioxide equivalents, converts emissions of methane and nitrous oxide into units of carbon oxide according to weights agreed by the IPCC).

Agriculture and the land-use sector uniquely also have the potential to offset these emissions through the process of carbon sequestration. Agricultural soils and peatlands can be managed in a way that absorbs carbon dioxide from the air, while changes in land use such as afforestation can also store carbon in the additional trees.

Finally, agriculture, as an activity depending on natural processes (rainfall, temperature, biodiversity, soils), will need to adapt to a changing climate. Some of these changes will be positive but others, such as the likelihood of greater frequency of extreme events such as heavy flooding or longer drought periods, will challenge farmers to change existing practices.

Agricultural emissions have fluctuated since national inventory figures were first collected in 1990, but they are now at the same level as they were in 1990 and are on an upward trend. Projections to 2040 by Teagasc and the Environmental Protection Agency predict that, on a business-as-usual scenario, absolute emissions will continue to increase. This trend is not in line with the national commitment to an approach to carbon neutrality in the agriculture and land use sector which does not compromise the capacity for sustainable food production. So, what can be done?

Continuing improvements in the carbon efficiency of agricultural production (by reducing emissions per unit of output) should continue to be an objective of policy. Voluntary initiatives such as Origin Green and farm advice based on the Carbon Navigator, as well as the Smart Farming Initiative, run jointly by the IFA and the Environmental Protection Agency, play an important role in raising awareness and highlighting steps that farmers can take on their farms. Robust monitoring of emission reductions is important to maintain the credibility of these schemes.

Teagasc has examined the technical options open to farmers to reduce emissions by developing a Marginal Abatement Cost Curve (Lanigan and Donnellan, 2018). The idea behind this curve is to rank all technical options according to their estimated cost of reducing emissions. Some options may have negative costs, meaning that it would increase farm profitability if farmers adopted them. Other options would require additional investment by farmers or would increase their costs.

Where the increase in costs is less than the assumed cost of continuing GHG emissions (as reflected, for example, in the price of emission allowances in the EU Emissions Trading Scheme or the level of carbon tax imposed on domestic businesses and households), it makes sense to adopt these options. Whether farmers should themselves pay these extra costs, or whether adoption of these practices should be subsidised by the taxpayer, is a political decision on how the burden should be shared in line with the principles of a just transition.

Teagasc identified around fourteen different technical options which, if adopted in full, could reduce agricultural emissions by around 3 million tonnes CO_2e in 2030 or a reduction of 15% on current levels. It estimated that a further four million tonnes CO_2 could be removed by 2030 through land use change, primarily afforestation at the rate of around seven thousand hectares per annum. It also noted that fossil fuel energy substitution by cultivating biofuel/bioenergy crops along with the adoption of anaerobic digesters to convert slurry and other organic materials and wastes into biogas could displace another two million tonnes CO_2 (though this saving would be recorded in the energy sector and not the agricultural sector in the national inventory accounts). It estimated that the cost of achieving this level of abatement would be less than €50 per tonne of CO_2e abated for most of the measures considered.

These figures assume that all farmers fully adopt the relevant measures. There is much evidence that the uptake of climate mitigation measures is usually much less than 100%. For example, planting rates for new forestry have fallen to 4–5,000 hectares per annum compared to the 7,000ha assumed in the Teagasc figures. For this reason, while it is important to pursue the search for efficient technical options to reduce emissions, we also need to pay attention to how farmers are incentivised to adopt these solutions.

Tackling emissions by improving carbon efficiency and reducing the carbon intensity per unit of output should be attractive to farmers because the measures taken often reduce unit costs and improve profitability at the same time. Indeed, there have been noticeable improvements in the emissions intensity of production over time (Buckley et al., 2019). However, overall agricultural output has increased at an even faster rate, so that the absolute level of emissions continues to rise. Additional efforts are therefore required.

Some parts of the answer are known. They include a greater area under forestry, some re-wetting of peatlands, more use of energy crops and agro-forestry, as well as greater attention to the provision of ecosystem services including biodiversity and flood management. The number of ruminant animals, particularly suckler cows producing beef, will also need to be reduced.

Raising animals for beef is widespread on Irish farms. Excluding farms with dairy cows, 93,000 farms out of a total of 140,000 keep cattle either for breeding (suckler cows) or rearing and fattening (calves from both the dairy and suckler cow herds). What is extraordinary is that, on average, none of these farms make money from breeding, buying and selling cattle. The Teagasc National Farm Survey shows that the entire farm income of these farms comes from agricultural policy payments under the CAP. These payments include area-based payments per hectare (decoupled payments often referred to as the 'cheque in the post'), additional payments to farms in areas facing natural constraints, and agri-environment payments to farmers who voluntarily enrol in such schemes. Yet successive incentive schemes have led to an increase in suckler cow numbers from half a million in the 1970s to around 1 million head today.

This provides a major transformation opportunity. There would be no cost to many farmers moving out of beef production provided their CAP payments are maintained. What is needed is to condition the CAP payments in such a way as to encourage farmers to take this step. What farmers decide to do with land freed up in this way should be up to them. Some farmers may opt to reduce stocking rates and to extensify, perhaps as part of an agri-environment scheme with an emphasis on low fertiliser use and encouraging biodiversity. Others may decide to plant trees, or to use part of their land for energy crops, or to use their land for recreational purposes or care farming. A huge effort will be required from the Teagasc research and advisory services to identify alternative opportunities for beef farmers, many of whom are elderly and in receipt of off-farm sources of income.

The national transition objective notes that progress towards climate neutrality in the agriculture and land use sectors should not compromise the capacity for sustainable food production, but a sector which is so dependent on subsidy (as well as very high tariff protection) cannot be said to be sustainable. A reduction in the suckler cow herd would lead to greater competition for cattle thus raising their price, which would help to underpin the livelihoods of those farmers who would remain in beef production.

The Oireachtas Joint Committee on Climate Action set up to consider the recommendations of the Citizens' Assembly has noted that greater opportunities will be available under the Commission's legal proposal for the CAP post 2020 to focus CAP payments on climate action (Oireachtas, 2019). Under the Commission's proposal, Ireland will be required to draw up a CAP plan showing how it intends to use CAP funding to achieve targets for a range of specific objectives, including climate mitigation and adaptation. The Joint Committee recommended that CAP funds should be used to fund priority measures for climate mitigation, biodiversity and carbon sequestration and storage.

If Ireland is to become a leader in climate change, it is essential that agricultural emissions are steadily reduced. This will require action on many fronts, including buy-in from farmers themselves, technical innovations that reduce emissions compared to current practices (for example, ways to lower methane emissions from ruminants or different fertiliser formulations that reduce nitrous oxide emissions), advances in measurement, monitoring and verification, changes in how land is used, and putting in place the appropriate incentives to make all of this happen.

Alan Matthews is professor emeritus of European Agricultural Policy at Trinity College, Dublin. He is a member of the Climate Change Advisory Council, but this chapter is written in his personal capacity and does not necessarily reflect the views of the council.

References

Buckley, C., Donnellan, T., Dillon, E., Hanrahan, K., Moran, B., & Ryan, M. (2019). *Teagasc National Farm Survey 2017 Sustainability Report.* Athenry: Teagasc Rural Economy Research Centre.

Lanigan, G., & Donnellan, T. (eds). (2018). *An Analysis of Abatement Potential of Greenhouse Gas Emissions in Irish Agriculture 2021–2030*. Oakpark: Teagasc.

Oireachtas. (2019). *Climate Change: A Cross-Party Consensus for Action.* Dublin: Report of the Joint Committee on Climate Action.

HUMAN INFLUENCES ON OUR DECLINING INSECT POLLINATORS

MARIA KIRRANE

If you talk to anyone who experienced driving a car along a country road on a summer's evening in the 1980s they will undoubtedly recount the mass of insect carcasses collected on the car's windscreen over the course of an average journey. Fast-forward to the present day and the situation has changed beyond recognition. Recent news items have carried with them stark warnings; in January 2019, the *Guardian* carried the stark headline: 'Insect Collapse: We are Destroying our Life Support Systems', in February the Irish national broadcaster, RTÉ, warned 'Insect Decline Could Cause Collapse of Nature'. The so-called 'windscreen phenomenon' is a very real manifestation of these alarming warnings. And this isn't just happening in Ireland; a recent global review of this trend, published in January of this year found that 40% of insect species are now threatened with extinction (Sánchez-Bayo & Wyckhuys, 2019). Among the most negatively impacted species are the lepidoptera (butterflies and moths) and the hymenoptera (wasps, bees, and ants).

As clear as our modern windscreens is the fact that the last two decades have brought immense changes across society as a whole. While our land continues to produce more and more food per hectare, the flora and fauna that were a part of the natural landscape, and our heritage, have changed significantly. One of the most striking examples on the island of Ireland has been the decline of over 90% in curlew numbers, an iconic Irish bird that feeds on terrestrial insects. Humanity's demand for food, water and natural resources are driving many of the processes that regulate the stability and resilience of our planet beyond their 'safe operating space' (Rockström et al., 2009). This in turn increases the risk to our environment of abrupt and irreversible change. The Stockholm Resilience Centre has undertaken significant work in quantifying these 'planetary boundaries' which include many of the processes that are driving our insect population declines (Rockström et al., 2009). For example, the same global review of insect declines lists the causes in descending order of importance as: habitat loss, pollution, introduced species and climate change (Sánchez-Bayo & Wyckhuys, 2019). These are not mutually exclusive. As the main source of declines, habitat destruction can take the form of both a loss of whole habitats or their fragmentation. The former results in a loss of suitable nesting sites and food sources, while the latter can cause populations to become isolated, thereby impacting on their breeding range and their ability to adapt, or respond geographically to other environmental pressures, for example climate change.

Turning to our local situation, Ireland is home to ninety-eight species of bee, the majority of which are solitary bees. Only one honey bee species is native to Ireland, but many more have been imported over the years by beekeepers. More than half of Ireland's bees have undergone substantial declines in their numbers since 1980; the distribution of forty-two species has declined by more than 50% (Fitzpatrick, Murray, Paxton, & Brown, 2006). Of the twenty species of bumblebee in the country, six are threatened with extinction, while of the seventy-seven species of solitary bee, twenty-four are threatened with extinction. In a 'stable' ecosystem, closely related species co-exist through occupying different niches (niche differentiation) or utilising different resources (resource differentiation) thus avoiding direct competition. If sudden changes occur over shorter timescales, in the variability of particular resources, this may increase competition between species (Higginson, 2017). In Ireland for example, later emerging species of bees are declining at a faster rate due to changes in grassland management regimes (Fitzpatrick, Murray, Paxton, Breen, et al., 2007).

To follow the headlines, we are entering a time of 'insect apocalypse', but what impact is that likely to have on life as we know it? Pollination is essentially the act of transferring a pollen grain from the male plant (or part thereof) to the female plant. While some plants achieve pollination through abiotic factors, for example wind, the vast majority require animal pollination. The world is home to about two hundred and seventy-five thousand species of flowering plant, this diversity believed to have emerged thanks to co-evolution between plants and their animal pollinators, which began over two hundred and fifty million years ago (Bruce, 2015). Mutualistic relationships evolved in which pollinators gain nectar for food or fragrance for mating while at the same time pollen grains are carried from flower to flower. Some of these relationships became so specialised that a single species plant came to rely on a single species of pollinator for this 'service'. If that pollinator is lost, so too is its specialist plant, impacting in turn on the herbivores that feed on that plant; think of a Jenga tower where more and more blocks are being removed, or to use the scientific term an 'extinction cascade'. In addition, these plants in turn provide many services to humans including food and medicines. Insects pollinate over 75% of the world's crop species, in some cases an insect pollinator is a required, while in others it serves to improve yield quality, for example oilseed rape (Bartomeus et al., 2014). In Ireland alone, this pollination service is worth €53 million annually to the Irish economy supporting the production of crops such as apples, tomatoes, strawberries and cucumbers (National Biodiversity Data Centre, 2015). The value of pollination is not confined to the kitchen table. While much of the attention to pollinator decline concentrates on food crops, as it is the most easily valued, loss of pollinators would have enormous 'ecological and evolutionary implications for plants, food webs, and ecosystem function' (Vanbergen & Insect Pollinators Initiative, 2013).

Intensive agriculture not only degrades habitat availability, but the provision of a safe and healthy environment for pollinators as well. There has been much debate over the years regarding the toxicity of agricultural pesticides in insects. One of the most controversial and hotly debated pesticides has been the 'neonicotinoid' pesticides. Neonicotinoids have been favoured in agriculture thanks to their 'systemic' action and the fact that they have low toxicity in vertebrates. However, during much of their use, relatively little was known of the sub-lethal effects on non-target organisms. Much of the scientific studies had been carried out in laboratory settings, failing to account for environmental conditions. In 2017, a landmark study was published which assessed damage to bees across two continents and confirmed that neonicotinoid pesticides negatively impacted pollinator health under realistic agricultural conditions (Woodcock et al., 2017). Therefore, an ironic situation emerges where chemicals used to improve crop yields may be impacting negatively on the pollinators required to pollinate them. Added to this is the fact that across an average intensively managed agricultural landscape multiple different chemical pesticides may be in use, leading to a 'cocktail effect' of toxicity. A trade-off emerges, the impacts of which in a changing global agricultural structure are unknown (Zimmermann & Stout, 2016). Faced with more and more evidence of a link between pesticides and bee health, in 2018 the EU issued a ban on neonicotinoid pesticides. This ban is an example of the EU's Precautionary Principle in action, a core principle of EU environmental law which supports intervention where there is uncertainty surrounding the supporting evidence.

While land-use changes and habitat loss are to blame for much of the decline in bumble bee species, the decline in our native honey bee tells a different story on how human consumption patterns have affected our natural world. Honey bees have long been the go-to pollinating insect as they can be managed by humans and they can also in some instances compensate for the loss of wild pollinators (Bartomeus et al., 2014). The European honey bee is the most widely cultivated and managed bee in the world, thought to have been introduced by European settlers as they colonised the New World. It is therefore also the most important pollinator of crops. Since the mid 1980s however, honey bees have been in decline due to the introduction of the invasive parasitic mite *Varroa destructor.* The mite, which was introduced from Asia in the 1960s feeds on the bee's haemolymph (effectively its blood) and spreads diseases that, in normal (non-parasitised) populations, would not affect them. Since it shifted host to the European honey bee, the Varroa mite has been found on every continent except Australia. The outcome has been the decimation of wild honey bee colonies so that, in the invaded range of the Varroa mite, honey bees only exist as managed colonies widely treated with chemical acaricides (chemicals designed to kill mites). The potential for synergistic 'cocktail' effects between these chemicals remains unknown. This decline in an economically important pollinator – to the extent that it is no longer a 'wild' species, existing solely in managed hives – highlights our need to maintain and even promote populations of our other one hundred wild pollinating species.

Like all sustainability challenges, the threats facing our insect pollinators are interconnected and complex. What is clear is that pollinator populations are declining, and human activity is to blame. Across the EU, various projects have been implemented to attempt to reverse these declines. In Ireland, the All-Ireland Pollinator Plan has developed guidance and action plans for multiple sectors including business, communities and agriculture. An integrated approach across urban and rural environments to improve the health and connectivity of habitats for insects is required. Recent EIP (European Innovation Partnership) projects funded across Ireland have dealt with the multiple factors leading to pollinator declines at local scales. Regional scale projects of this kind could be supported to ensure the value of these projects is not hampered by their isolation. In addition, the growth of urban agriculture and green infrastructure across European cities should be done in such a way as to support diverse insect populations. The impact of these initiatives needs to be determined.

Maria Kirrane is sustainability officer at University College Cork.

References

Bartomeus, I., Potts, S.G., Steffan-Dewenter, I., Vaissière, B.E., Woyciechowski, M., Krewenka, K.M., ... Bommarco, R. (2014). 'Contribution of Insect Pollinators to Crop Yield and Quality Varies with Agricultural Intensification'. *PeerJ*, 2, 328. Available at: doi:10.7717/peerj.328

Bruce, T. (2015). 'Interplay Between Insects and Plants: Dynamic and Complex Interactions That Have Coevolved Over Millions of Years but Act in Milliseconds'. *Journal of Experimental Botany*, 66(2), 455–465. Available at: https://doi.org/10.1093/jxb/eru391

Fitzpatrick, Ú., Murray, T.E., Paxton, R.J., Breen, J., Cotton, D., Santorum, V., & Brown, M.J. (2007). 'Rarity and Decline in Bumblebees – A Test of Causes and Correlates in the Irish Fauna'. *Biological Conservation*, 136(2), 185–194. Available at: https://doi.org/10.1016/j.biocon.2006.11.012

Fitzpatrick, Ú., Murray, T., Paxton, R., & Brown, M. (2006). The State of Ireland's Bees. *Environment & Heritage Service*. Available at: http://www.biodiversityireland.ie/wordpress/wp-content/uploads/The-state-of-Irelands-Bees.pdf

Higginson, A.D. (2017). 'Conflict Over Non-Partitioned Resources May Explain Between-Species Differences in Declines: The Anthropogenic Competition Hypothesis'. *Behavioral Ecology and Sociobiology*. Available at: https://doi.org/10.1007/s00265-017-2327-z

National Biodiversity Data Centre. (2015). *All-Ireland Pollinator Plan, 2015–2020*. Available at: https://pollinators.ie/

Rockström, J., Steffen, W.L., Noone, K., Persson, Å., Chapin III, F.S., Lambin, E., ... & Nykvist, B. (2009). 'Planetary Boundaries: Exploring the Safe Operating Space for Humanity'. *Ecology and Society*, 14(2): 32. Available at: http://www.ecologyandsociety.org/vol14/iss2/art32/

Sánchez-Bayo, F., & Wyckhuys, K.A. (2019). 'Worldwide Decline of the Entomofauna: A Review of its Drivers'. *Biological Conservation*, 232, 8–27. Available at: https://doi.org/10.1016/j.biocon.2019.01.020

Vanbergen, A.J., & Insect Pollinators Initiative. (2013). 'Threats to an Ecosystem Service: Pressures on Pollinators'. *Frontiers in Ecology and the Environment*, 11(5), 251–259. Available at: doi:10.1890/120126

Woodcock, B.A., Bullock, J.M., Shore, R.F., Heard, M.S., Pereira, M.G., Redhead, J., ... & Peyton, J. (2017). 'Country-Specific Effects of Neonicotinoid Pesticides on Honey Bees and Wild Bees'. *Science*, 356(6345), 1393–1395.

Zimmermann, J., & Stout, J.C. (2016). 'Underestimating Neonicotinoid Exposure: How Extent and Magnitude May Be Affected by Land-Use Change'. *Environmental Science and Pollution Research*, 23, 7050.

SUSTAINABILITY AND TRANSPORT: LEADING THE COMMUNITY, NOT DRIVING IT

CONOR FAUGHNAN

One of nature's oddest quirks is the massive detour taken by the laryngeal nerve of the giraffe. Instead of running directly from the brain to the larynx the nerve takes a 4.5 metre detour down the neck and back again to loop around an artery. The result works but is enormously inefficient. We know the reason. Evolution over time saw the neck lengthening in tiny increments. At each stage, there was no way to 're-wire' the living animal, so the nerve lengthened along with the neck.

Cities, systems, societies and cultures have a similar pattern to their development. Architects and planners do not have the luxury of a blank canvas. They get to make incremental changes, big and small, to the living canvas of the active society. Transport evolved with us, adding layers and new technologies. Better transport over longer distances means you can commute. Cities can get bigger and more efficient. Congestion then takes back those gains. The basic way to power transport was figured out in the nineteeth century and has not changed much since because it worked.

We dig up the fossilised remains of living organisms, often fighting each other for control of it. We build large factories to refine it into volatile liquid. We then make machines that burn the liquid in a series of controlled explosions, venting waste heat, organic compounds and vast amounts of CO_2 out the rear. Your machine rolls beautifully down the road and the design is so elegant that you can go in total comfort while listening to music and traffic reports.

There are two or three fundamental problems with this approach. Firstly, it is finite. It took nature three hundred and fifty million years to make all of the world's oil; mankind has been using it for one hundred and fifty years and half of it is gone. The second problem is the tail-pipe. No need for detail here: fossil fuel use is causing a build-up of CO_2 which is warming the planet and changing the climate in ways that we are still scrambling to fully understand. There is a third problem around the quality of life not for the planet but for ourselves. When you zoom in to the individual we are all busy to the point of being frantic. We have needs and wants and desires that, once survival is taken care of, are all about where we are in the human society. We live individual lives. I may care a lot about the planet but I am likely to care more about good schools for my kids. I may act powerfully on things that matter to me and that are within my control.

Our cities, and certainly our Irish cities, reflect this. They are grown like weeds rather than planned like gardens. Development follows the line of best commercial return to provide the housing that we have culturally made the norm. We have made the already difficult challenge of transport even worse. We commute because it is normal. We drive to the gym or the GAA pitch because that is what you do.

A congested city is good for no-one. We can all agree that we do not want poisoned air. No one is in favour of global unpredictable climate change. But getting us to think long term and globally is difficult.

Two approaches tend to be taken. The first involves educating people about the bigger picture. On climate change specifically, there is an abundance of evidence to turn to. We can talk also about the collective effect of seven billion humans on the natural environment.

The second approach is to incentivise. You cannot truly make someone do something, you can only make them want to. If you want more electric cars on the road to replace fossil fuels, then you should make it as easy as possible for the ordinary consumer to make that choice.

Encouraging global thinking is great. It makes perfect sense to do it. But like the town planner's job, it is not that straight forward. The human world is a noisy place. Real issues compete with an information overload from all directions. Fake news, real news, Kim Kardashian's bum, snake-oil salesmen, anti-vaxers and sinister people surfing to power on deliberately stoked anger and confusion.

Climate issues get treated with the same glibness and reduced to soundbites. We thought democracy meant that you are entitled to your own opinion; it has come to mean you are entitled to your own facts. When you've had a homeopath lecture you on climate science you can appreciate the irony.

Even with great good will and clarity it is often hard for citizens to draw a real connection between their local choices and the global challenges we face. Will it really make a difference if I don't use a plastic bag this time or take the bus to work?

As a very tiny part of a very tiny country, am I doing any more than just making a virtuous gesture; something to make me feel good about myself when I'm sipping Brazilian coffee from a single-use cup?

If we want to make changes that are going to stick, then it is essential for the community of real people to buy into it. It gets toxic when people feel patronised, picked upon or blamed.

In rural Ireland especially, there is a genuine feeling that wealthy suburban liberals are happy to use rural hardship to pay for their eco-gestures. No problem hitting the beef industry, or the diesel price. No mention of the carbon cost of the skinny-Frappuccino. These are the same people who cried wolf before. Nuclear power was bad and then oil was bad. We were told to buy diesel cars, now we are told it is our fault because we did.

Perhaps every single one of those thoughts is unfair. But it is important to engage them because if we are going to change it has to be by agreement, together. Too often we have people who are only willing to listen to those who agree with them. They compete by trying to outdo each other ideologically, treating those with different views as 'deplorables'. It gets us nowhere.

People will follow their own individual interest. They will rationalise and compartmentalise, but, in the end, they will do what is best for themselves. It is just what happens. It shows in economics, in sociology, in all of human history. You can wish it was different but that is like wishing that water would make a moral choice to flow uphill.

As a cure for this sort of cynicism I can highly recommend going along to the BT Young Scientists' Exhibition, held every January in Dublin's RDS. Just to chat to the young students and to get the depth of their passion and their understanding is terrific. Every year there are brilliant and original projects included and they reflect modern social concerns as seen by young people. It is evident that the brightest and best of the coming generation care deeply about climate and environmental issues.

It is seeping into our social values but it is taking time. Those who take the climate challenge most seriously are often passionately anxious to act, to do something right now. I understand the frustration. But for policies beyond gestures to stick, it takes time.

If you talk to a young person now about LGBTI issues, for example, you will hear a very different vocabulary and level of awareness compared to ten or twenty years ago. It has become mainstream; core societal values have changed. You will still hear all sorts of views but undeniably the centre of gravity has shifted.

Something similar has happened over the years with road safety. In the 1990s, a broadly tolerant Ireland did not wish to be over-policed and traffic offences were thought of as very much misdemeanours. Alcohol limits were high and the typical driver would feel hard done by if a Garda did not send him home with a warning instead of charging him.

At the time in Europe and elsewhere there was a growing determination to treat all road deaths as preventable and to oblige governments, manufacturers and citizens to reduce the numbers. Ireland's first road safety strategy was adopted in 1998 and it set the country on a journey of continuous improvement. In 1997, there were four hundred and seventy-two people killed on Irish roads. In 2018, that figure was one hundred and forty-nine.

The success of road safety policies is no longer seriously debated but if in 1998 we had attempted to introduce all of the measures that are now standard the project would have lost public support and failed. Speed cameras, penalty points, random breath checks, actual prosecutions instead of slaps on the wrist; these were all new.

Not that road safety is perfect. There is often the tendency to cherry-pick data, to overstate the case for certain measures and in so doing alienate support. The real data on alcohol is bad enough without having to exaggerate it and that can be counter-productive.

There is often political cynicism as well. Successive Irish transport ministers always want to bring in new laws. It is much easier and makes for a better press release than actually labouring away at enforcing the laws we have. But on the whole, warts and all, the road safety strategy has worked.

Can we make a similar success of a clean and sustainable transport policy? To bring broad social support along with us on the journey we need to speak, act, legislate and plan in sympathy with the world as it is now, not the world as we would wish it. For some that is a cop-out; it is not radical enough or urgent enough. It denies that the world must change.

It is the pragmatists who achieve change though, not the zealots. Take the small example of carbon taxes. A large part of the population chose to buy diesel cars because they were told at the time that this was a cleaner choice and tax incentives channelled them that way. If we choose now to target those people for tax increases they will resist. They will think *Frappuccinos* again and they will feel victimised.

These measures force divisive conversations, identity-politics and dialogues of the deaf. We should not separate the world into those people who get the issue and those who selfishly refuse to. Real life and real people are more complicated than that. It is more sensible and fairer to understand their needs and work with them. We can pick things that we all agree on, and then we can design our social incentives so that people are naturally inclined to go for those things.

There are simple and humble measures which, unlike the politician, we can get on with instead of grandstanding. The provision of cycle lanes and parking in our towns for example, and giving employers a tax break to put in bike racks and showers.

These are things that are practical, cheap, universally supportable and most importantly, victimless.

Electric vehicles (EVs) have fantastic potential. There are problems that they do not solve, like congestion. They will add substantially to electricity demand at a time when we make dirty electricity for a grid that is not big enough. But we can work on those problems. What EVs do give us is a vision of what future transport can be. Clean, emission-free movement with the potential to be completely sustainable and renewable.

They also point the slow engine of big capital in the direction that we want it to go. Like water flowing downhill, big capital will seek out the best return. It does not need to chase oil but it does not have a conscience. It will always go where it is channelled so you may as well design for that instead of wishing it were different.

For drivers, EVs are quickly growing in popularity. This is not because they are eco-friendly and not because they signal virtue to the world. It is because they are great cars. That is the way to do it.

These are national conversations that will continue. It may well happen that in ten years' time as I drive my EV through town I will have Frappuccino-zealots waving at me about the deplorable way in which lithium is mined. No doubt the world will still face challenges on climate, sustainability, and social justice in the human world.

But I have confidence in my community and my society. We will talk, we will grumble and we will argue, but together we will get there.

Conor Faughnan is director of consumer affairs at the AA. He is the AA's media spokesman on matters related to roads, transport, safety and motoring consumer issues.

SECTION FIVE

SELFISHNESS, ALTRUISM AND RESILIENCE

> Every man must decide
> whether he will walk
> in the light of creative
> altruism or in the
> darkness of destructive
> selfishness.

Martin Luther King, Jr

INSTITUTIONALISED SELFISHNESS AND CRUELTY IN SOCIETY

CATHERINE CONLON

> 'In a free society, government reflects the soul of its people. If people want change at the top, they will have to live in different ways. Our major social problems are not the cause of our decadence. They are a reflection of it.'
>
> **Cal Thomas**

Selfishness is the modus operandi in totalitarian regimes that disregards the rights and freedoms of the individual. It is also manifest in democratic countries though – as institutionalised selfishness – where profit is more important than the attendent damage to the population in which the organisation operates.

This applies to industries and companies that have the power to influence governments to modify laws and regulations to suit their own needs and maximise profit.

This is evident in the large amounts of money spent on polished advertising campaigns to hide the potential harmful effects of products or activities, whatever the price to humanity or the planet.

It includes paying small fortunes to lawyers to prolong law suits indefinitely, to discourage victims of their activities with limited resources from pursuing justice.

These groups achieve ongoing economic growth and wealth; and exploit workers while passing environmental costs to society. Activity such as this is beginning to be recognised as 'moral deprivation' where the moral compass of the financial and multinational sector is skewed.

World renowned scientists close to political parties in the United States have, for decades, led disinformation campaigns, allowing public opinion to be swayed against the scientific evidence. Examples of successfully influenced campaigns, include the link between tobacco and cancer, fumes from the coal industry and acid rain, and the role of chlorofluorocarbons (CFCs) in the destruction of the ozone layer (Oreskes & Conway, 2012).

In terms of tobacco, this evidence for the link between tobacco and premature death (six hundred million per year) has achieved widespread acceptance in the developed world, leading to strict regulation in terms of advertising and promotion. As a result, the tobacco industry has now turned its attention on developing countries, particularly in Africa and Asia.

Food and Drink

The power of this industry is apparent in its ability to prevent change in legislation that might affect the profit margin, despite the clear benefits to society in physical, as well as social and economic, terms of introducing legislation to curb overall consumption of alcohol, binge drinking and consumption of obesogenic food.

In the United States, consumers spend approximately $1 trillion annually on food, which accounts for nearly 10% of the gross domestic product (GDP), while 6% of exports revolve around food, accounting for another $56 billion. More than 16.5 million people are employed in the US food industry. Almost all of that consumption includes some form of sugar. This product is too valuable to the economy for the government to consider significant legislative change that would curb consumption.

In 2002, a policy forum was called by the World Health Organisation (WHO) and the Food and Agriculture Organisation of the United Nations (FAO), to address the role of nutrition in disease.

The resultant publication, *TRS 916*, called for limiting added sugar to less than 10% of the total calories in the diet (WHO, 2003).

The American Food Manufacturer's Group began lobbying in Washington. The American Sugar Association threatened to 'exercise every avenue available to expose the dubious nature of the report.' This resulted in a letter from the Department of Health to the WHO, denying any evidence for the link between junk food and obesity. This was followed by a threat to withhold the $406 million annual US contribution to the WHO unless *TRS 916* was repealed. Inevitably, this is what happened.

Climate Change

Disinformation campaigns in relation to global warming are ongoing. Initially, US scientists – allied to political parties – claimed it didn't exist, then it was a natural phenomenon and finally, if it continues to increase, we will have to develop systems to adapt to this new era. They do this by challenging the results of peer reviewed papers and accusing researchers of manipulating the data. They are armed with the support of industry who fear regulation of their activities and by the support of US presidents including, in the past, Ronald Reagan, George Bush Snr and George Bush Jnr. They also succeed in manipulating a media in search of new headlines and diverse opinions (Oreskes & Conway, 2012).

The current US president, Donald Trump, has pulled the US out of the Paris Climate Agreement and consistently enthuses about the virtues of coal. Ireland is not off the hook either. The current administration has cut subventions to public transport, allowed the dairy herd to increase by four hundred thousand and issued new licences for oil and gas exploration. Now the government wants to move the cost of climate change onto the people with a carbon tax on fossil fuels, despite the evidence that carbon taxes do not deliver anything like the reductions in CO_2 that are needed.

Recent research by the International Panel on Climate Change shows that we need to reduce CO_2 emissions by 45% in the next decade and to zero by 2050. A reasonable way to achieve this would be for world governments to set legally enforceable limits on corporations responsible for most of the emissions and a tax on corporate profits to fund a major investment in renewable technology, as opposed to a socially regressive tax that targets the consumption of individuals.

On top of this, petroleum products are defined as inelastic by economists, meaning that individuals tend to stick with them, regardless of their prices. This is because they are essential for daily living and hard to replace with alternatives.

The academic evidence also shows that carbon taxes are not hugely effective; the most positive results showing CO_2 emissions reductions of between 5–9% which is nowhere near enough. More importantly, the carbon tax shifts responsibility from the major corporate polluters and onto consumers. The problem with this is that one hundred global corporations are responsible for 71% of all emissions through the products they place on the market (O'Boyle, 2019).

In Ireland, households account for 15% of all emissions while agriculture is responsible for 32%. Despite this, the Irish government is committed to increasing the dairy herd by 22% over the next decade and have resisted calls for major investment in public transport, while continuing to issue licences for exploration for oil and gas. This demonstrates hypocrisy as well as institutionalised selfishness in policy, allowing carbon emissions to continue to rise to maximise profits while using the carbon tax as a method of appeasing national climate change concerns.

If the government was really interested in tackling change, while protecting the most vulnerable members of society, it would consider measures such as: major investment in renewable energy; free public transport; a shift in agricultural policy from dairy to forestry; public housing; to reduce transport costs and emissions; government spending to incentivise retrofitting of houses; an end to fossil fuel exploration; and a move to a carbon neutral economy by 2035 through legally binding emission limits (O'Boyle, 2019).

Cruelty in the Animal Industry

Evidence that society has normalised cruelty is apparent by the way we treat animals. The most obvious example of this is the meat industry. In wealthy parts of the world – such as the United States, Europe and more recently China – 99% of the animals are kept in industrial breeding grounds where their brief lives involve constant suffering, made possible because animals are considered objects of consumption.

Slaughterhouses maximise the ability to kill animals quickly, efficiently and with minimum expense. Industrial animal production systems almost everywhere escape the laws protecting animals from abuse. Since caring for weak animals is costly, animals that are too weak to follow others into slaughterhouses are allowed to die of hunger or thirst. This occurs on a daily basis (Foer, 2009).

Economic competition forces the rate of animal kills per hour. The speed of the conveyer belt in slaughterhouses allows over one thousand animals to be dealt with per hour.

The vet's role is to maximise profit. In many countries, animals are filled with antibiotics and growth hormones to maximise growth. Eighty per cent of the antibiotics produced in the United States are used in the animal industry (Foer, 2009).

The fate of chickens is almost as bad. Globally, fifty billion chickens are slaughtered annually. Overcrowding leads to aberrant behaviour such as birds plucking their own feathers, aggressive pecking and cannibalism. Artificial accelerated growth is likened to a child reaching three hundred and thirty pounds by the age of ten.

Chickens are kept in semi darkness to limit fighting. Wounding is minimised by chopping off their beaks, the remaining stumps frequently developing painful neuromas (Breward & Gentle, 1985).

Slaughterhouses are supposed to stun chickens in an electrified bath. Use of weak voltage to save money frequently results in chickens being scalded alive. Male chicks are destroyed – this involves being sucked through a series of pipes onto an electrical plate. Others are sent fully conscious through macerators (Foer, 2012).

Pigs are tied by a leash in stalls to prevent them moving around. Their tails are cut off to prevent them biting each other's tails off. Males are castrated without anaesthetic. Piglets that don't grow up fast enough are 'thumped': picked up by their hind legs and smashed off a concrete floor.

Calves are locked into stalls that prevent their natural sleeping position, head tucked under, as well as preventing them turning around or licking themselves. Their food is deliberately kept low in iron as consumers like 'pale' meat (Foer, 2009).

The Meat Industry, Global Poverty and Ecological Sustainability

Apart from the way in which animals are treated for human consumption, the meat industry has direct connotations in relation to global poverty and ecological sustainability. Industrial breeding contributes 14.5% of greenhouse gas emissions linked to human activities. This is second only to construction and before transportation (Zevenhoven, 2015). Production of 1kg of meat requires 10kg of food that could be used to feed poor countries (Ensminger, 1991). The breeding industry accounts of 60% of the land available globally and consumes 45% of all the water destined for food production. The land is used for pasture and grain. Reducing meat production by 30% could prevent 14% of deaths globally. One hectare of land can feed fifty vegetarians or two carnivores. To produce 1kg of meat requires the same land surface as is required to produce 80kg of apples, 160kg of potatoes, or 200kg of tomatoes (Rifkin, 2012).

One acre of grain produces five times more protein than the same acre to produce meat. An acre of vegetables produces ten times more protein than the same acre to produce meat (Doyle, 1985).

The breeding industry consumes 750 million tonnes of wheat and corn every year – enough to feed adequately the 1.4 billion poorest human beings (Worldwatch, 2015).

To obtain one calorie of beef by intensive breeding, eight to twenty-six calories of plant food are required which could otherwise have been consumed by humans. This type of agriculture has been described as 'a protein factory in reverse' (Foer, 2009).

Eating meat is the preserve of wealthy countries at the expense of the poor. The more wealth accrued, the more meat is consumed. Average annual consumption of meat in the United States is 120kg compared to 2.5kg in India. Globally, meat production increased by a factor of five from 1950 to 2000. A further doubling of consumption is predicted between 2000 and 2050 (FAO, 2006).

The meat industry consumes more than one-third of global grain production. This competition for grains between man and animal increases the price of grain – further impacting negatively on the poorest populations (FAO, 2006).

In Central America, in order to produce one hamburger, seventeen square metres of virgin forest are transformed into pasture and 75kg of plant and animals are destroyed.

Tropical forests cover 720 million hectares and harbour half of the biodiversity of the planet. Over 200 million hectares have been destroyed since 1950 – mainly to make room for pasture or cattle farms (Boyan, 2005).

Meat production also has a significant impact on water reserves. Lack of fresh drinking water is a global threat. Forty per cent of the world's population has insufficient water both in quantity and quality as 70% of the world's fresh water is polluted. Over three million children die annually from gastroenteritis caused by drinking dirty water (Francis & Orbhabor, 2017).

Production of 1kg of meat requires fifty times more water than production of 1kg of wheat (Bergstrom, 1973). It is estimated that half of the world's fresh drinking water is consumed by the production of meat and meat products. Intensive animal breeding, including fish farming, is also a significant cause of water pollution. This demand is exhausting aquifers throughout the world, even more so in recent decades with the impact of climate change on the poorest, most vulnerable populations. This figure is predicted to get even worse as the quantity of water used by industrial animal breeding is expected to rise by 50% by 2050 (Rosengrant & Meijer, 2002).

More than one-third of the global production of grains is destined for the meat industry, as is one-third of the global production of fish. This competition for grains between man and animal increases the price of grain, which impacts negatively on the poorest populations.

In terms of greenhouse gas emissions, the impact of meat production is stark. Meat production produces fifty times more greenhouse gases per kilogramme than that of 1kg of wheat, leading to a global figure of 14.5% of all gas emissions responsible for climate change, being surpassed only by the construction industry and being responsible for more globally than the transport industry (Gerber, 2013).

Greenhouse gases are mainly due to three gases: methane, carbon dioxide and nitrous oxide. Methane gas contributes twenty times more to the greenhouse gas effect than carbon dioxide. Between 15% and 20% of methane emissions globally are linked to livestock breeding. In two centuries, the concentration of methane in the atmosphere has doubled (Zongkai, 2012).

The meat industry has been responsible for a significant portion of carbon dioxide emissions as well. Industrial meat production depends on mechanised agriculture, on the use of petroleum-based fertilisers, as well as on deforestation which prevents the resorption of carbon dioxide from the atmosphere.

Nitrous oxide is the most aggressive of greenhouse gases: three hundred and twenty times more active than carbon dioxide. It is also very stable, lasting for more than one hundred and twenty years in the atmosphere. The main source of nitrous oxide is the spread of fertiliser, the degradation of the fertiliser in the soil, as well as the waste products of livestock breeding – 65% of nitrous oxide emissions are the result of livestock breeding (FAO, 2006).

Animal waste is a significant source of water pollution, polluting waters more than all other sources combined. Excrement produces ammonia that pollutes waterways and seashores and causes algal invasions that stifle aquatic life.

Intensive fishing is leading to the extinction of numerous fish types, destroying a fragile ecosystem that has taken thousands of years to develop. It is estimated that the quantities harvested globally are vastly underestimated when the quantities are declared.

Industrial fishing is also characterised by immense waste. Shrimp trawlers throw 80–90% of sea creatures caught in one deep sea trawl overboard. This represents twenty-six pounds of sea creatures destroyed for every pound of shrimp produced. In the case of tuna, one hundred and forty-five other fish species are regularly discarded while catching tuna (Environmental Justice Foundation, 2010).

Persistent organic pollutants accumulate in the fatty tissues of animals (and farmed fish that are fed on animal proteins) and enter the food chain. These molecules are carcinogenic and toxic to the developing nervous system of a human foetus as well as young children.

In relation to antibiotics, 80% of antibiotics employed are used in the production of industrially bred meat products. These products are added to food and 75% of them are later found in rivers, soil and drinking water producing antibiotic resistance in humans (Foer, 2012).

The meat industry has been shown to be a vastly inefficient source of protein and calories and a contributor to global poverty in terms of the quantities of grain, vegetables and water required to sustain it; moreover, it is a significant contributor to global warming in terms of greenhouse gas emissions, second only to construction and contributing more emissions than the transport sector.

Reducing meat consumption could provide significant increases in grain provision for poor people, as well as effectively contributing to the fight against climate change, leading to more fresh water availability globally and vastly reduced pollution of freshwater supplies. It would also contribute to the fight against anti-microbial resistance.

A worldwide tendency towards a vegetable diet is considered essential to fight global hunger as well as an energy deficit and the worst impact of climate change. It is considered the easiest and most feasible option in terms of bringing about significant reductions in greenhouse gases in the shortest time period.

International cooperation on a global scale to reduce meat consumption is a potentially effective tool to slow down global warming and eradicate poverty, even before alteration in travel patterns or construction are considered.

Catherine Conlon is director of health and nutrition at Safefood, the all-island organisation that provides advice on food safety, healthy eating and food hygiene for consumers.

References

Bergstrom, G. (1973). *Harvesting the Earth*. New York: Abelard-Schuman.

Boyan, S. (2005). 'How Our Food Choices Can Help Save the Environment'. *Earth Save*. Available at: www.earthsave.org/environment/foodchoices.htm.

Breward, J., & Gentle, M. (1985). 'Neuroma formation and Abnormal Afferent Nerve Discharges After Partial Beak Amputation in Poultry'. *Experimentia*, 41(9):1132–1134.

Doyle, J. (1985). *Altered Harvest: Agriculture, Genetics and the Fate of the World's Food Supply*, 2nd ed., New York: Viking.

Ensminger, M. (1991). *Animal Science Digest*. Danville, Ill.: Interstate Publishers.

Food and Agriculture Organization. (2006). World Agriculture Towards 2015/2030. Rome: FAO.

Environmental Justice Foundation Charitable Trust. (2003). *Squandering the Seas: How shrimp trawling is threatening ecological integrity and food security around the world*. London: Environmental Justice Foundation.

Foer, J. (2009). *Eating Animals*. Boston: Back Bay Books.

Francis, A., & Orbhabor, B. (2017). 'The Public Health Implications of Pathogens in Polluted Aquatic Systems: A Review'. *Tropical Freshwater Biology*, 25(1):85.

Gerber, P.J. (2013). *Tackling Climate Change Through Livestock: A Global Assessment of Emissions and Mitigations Opportunities*. Rome: Food and Agriculture Organisation of the United Nations (FAO).

O'Boyle, B. (2019). 'Carbon Taxes Won't Stop Climate Change – We Need More Radical Action'. *The Guardian*, 26/03/2019.

Oreskes, N., & Conway, E. (2012). *Merchants of Doubt*. London: Bloomsbury.

Rifkin, J. (2012). *La Troisième Révolution Industrielle*. Paris: Les liens qui Libèrant.

Rosengrant, M., & Meijer, S. (2002). 'Appropriate Food Policies and Investments Could Reduce Child Malnutrition by 43% in 2020'. *The Journal of Nutrition*, 132(11):3437–3440.

World Health Organisation. (2003). *Diet, Nutrition and the Prevention of Chronic Disease*. Geneva: WHO.

Worldwatch Institute. (2015). *State of the World 2015: Confronting Hidden Threats to Sustainability*. Washington: Island Press.

Zevenhoven, R. (2015). 'Understanding Greenhouses Gases: Mission Being Accomplished'. *Greenhouses Gases: Science and Technology*, 5(6):695–696.

Zongkai. (2012). 'Greenhouse Gas Emissions: Quantifying Methane Emissions from Livestock'. *American Journal of Engineering and Applied Sciences*, 5(1):1–8.

TOWARDS AN ALTRUISTIC SOCIETY

CATHERINE CONLON

> Cooperation and partnership are the only route that offers any hope of a better future for all humanity.
>
> **Kofi Annan**

Cooperation is the creative force that drives evolution. It is recognised as the prerequisite to the construction of complex levels of organisation (Ricard, 2013). This is in contrast to modern economic theory that is founded on the existence of selfish agents devoted to maximising their own interests.

Human beings – by virtue of their language, their capacity for empathy and their vast range of emotions – are naturally social beings. This capacity for socialisation is not generally factored into public and economic policy. Ireland has a reputation globally for being one of the most social and hospitable nations in the world. It is these social and gregarious traits that allow us to thrive. And yet, much of the competitive individualism of modern society is at the core of addictive behaviour in terms of diet, alcohol, drugs and sexual deviance and contribute to anxiety, depression, obesity and lack of physical and mental well-being. At the individual level, competition poisons emotional and social links.

In strongly competitive societies, individuals do not trust one another, worry about their safety and constantly seek to promote their own interests and social status without much concern for others. Donald Trump, the United States president, with his America First, anti-immigration policy and consistent refusal to accept the evidence of climate change in the interests of American economic policy, is an obvious example of this mental inflexibility.

The opposite occurs in cooperative societies; individuals trust in one another and are prepared to devote time and resources to others. This sets in motion a virtuous cycle of solidarity and reciprocity that nurtures harmonious relationships and leads to low levels of crime and deviant behaviour (Neapolitan, 1999).

Trust is the essence of a civilised society and concomitant physical and mental well-being. As recognised by Martin Luther King, Jnr, 'We must learn to live together as brothers or perish together as fools.'

Education

A key ingredient for cooperation and understanding to flourish between communities is education. Studies that have looked at what most people want for their children see a number of recurring aspirations: happiness, self-confidence, health, satisfaction and love – in other words, physical and mental well-being (Seligman, 2011).

Yet when we look at what is being taught in school, we see that it is centred around other qualities: language, maths skills, discipline, success, work ethic. These skills are important, but school could also be a vital repository of other skills: psychological flexibility, resilience, ways of achieving well-being and self-fulfilment – skills that teach individuals to be the best version of themselves.

Modern education, with its focus on success and individualism, is not a focus for learning human values: of emotional intelligence and of working together. Researchers focusing on the pressures placed on children to succeed have suggested that this pressure – and the vulnerability it can activate in the event of failure – is among the factors contributing to high levels of depression and suicide among young people in developed countries (Seligman, 2011).

Imagine the transformational attitudinal change that could potentially emerge if education globally focused on psychological and mental flexibility and emotional balance; and in particular an understanding of the interdependence of human beings.

Fear of imposing values causes many educators to prefer a morally neutral approach – thinking it is not the school's role to impose moral preferences. But it is possible to inspire in children a constructive approach to benevolence, cooperation and integrity. Without direction, children will look to other compasses for a value system – notably social media or other media outlets with their focused message of consumerism and individualism, as well as casual violence. Teachers are in a unique position to influence the moral compass of their students and, in many cases, this has a lifelong impact.

Cooperative education is a model that is conducive to emphasising the benefits of an altruistic approach. This model organises children of varying levels of ability into groups – with a view to letting the most advanced help those with difficulties. This model suggests that children who find learning easy are filled with a sense of responsibility to those struggling to understand, rather than feeling superior to others as happens with a system driven by constant testing. On top of this, the spirit of group camaraderie, and the absence of intimidating judgemental influences, inspires confidence and the will to do their best (Plety, 1996).

Children in cooperating groups of similar ability have been found to come up with new ways of solving problems that previously had left them feeling marginalised and overwhelmed.

This form of learning has been found to lead to an increase in emotional intelligence, moral awareness, new friendships and better relations with teachers. Crucially, children have better psychological health, greater self-confidence and greater enjoyment of learning. It also leads to lower levels of discrimination (racist and sexist), delinquency, bullying and drug addiction (Johnson & Johnson, 1999).

Harari (2018) argues that schools should switch to teaching 'the four Cs': critical thinking, communication, collaboration and creativity. More broadly, schools should downplay technical skills and emphasise general purpose life skills. In particular, the ability to deal with change, to learn new things and to preserve mental balance in unfamiliar situations.

Inequality

Society has, at its core, a duty not to neglect those who are suffering. It cannot prevent inequality from arising but it can prevent it from persisting. A society that has altruism as its core value will ensure that equality is redressed along with lack of opportunity and access to healthcare and education.

Inequality can exist in terms of territory (rich and poor regions), economy (wealth and poverty in one region); sociology (ways of life) or in health (access to medical and technological advances or long waiting lists for healthcare). Territorial inequality is exacerbated by climate change as poorer regions are most vulnerable to extremes of climate in terms of heat, drought, flooding and wind.

Inequality can also exist in education, working conditions, justice systems (presence of corruption) and taxation (existence of tax havens).

Countries that have equality at their core strive to uphold social justice, while in the most unequal societies, financial and political institutions are engaged just as energetically in maintaining an unequal status quo.

Economic inequality is on the increase globally. In the US, the richest 1% own 40% of the wealth compared to 13% twenty-five years ago (Wolff, 2017). For thirty years, 90% of Americans saw their income increase by 15% while the wealthiest 1% saw their income increase by 150%. Contrary to the claims of libertarians, wealth at the top of the ladder stays there and does not trickle down to create a more equal, dynamic society.

In Europe, the level of inequality is not as high but it is rising. In countries with the lowest levels of inequality, such as Scandinavia, the richest 10% earn about six times more than the poorest 10% (OECD, 2014).

What is less well known is that income inequality slows growth and triggers financial crises. The income inequality gap is at its highest in thirty years in most OECD countries with the richest 10% of the OECD population earning nine and a half times more than the poorest 10% (OECD, 2014) This contrasts to a ratio of 7:1 in the 1980s. This long-term increase in income inequality has slowed economic growth because low-income families have insufficient income to invest in education and health.

Tax and social protection schemes, which play a major role in easing the levels of inequality brought about by free market capitalism, have in many countries ceased to be effective in the last fifteen years. This is because libertarian capitalist economies aim to reduce the role of government as well as reducing social welfare as much as possible.

At the same time, many countries have cut the top tax rate for people with the highest incomes. The OECD highlights the need for governments to revise fiscal policy so that the best off in society play an equal role in shouldering the tax burden.

Based on research drawn from major international organisations, including the United Nations, the results demonstrate that for each health and social indicator (physical health, mental health, school success rate, obesity, drug addiction, violence and murder), the results are significantly worse where inequality is highest (Wilkinson & Pichett, 2010).

This relationship exists when the results are confined to developed countries with better results for all indicators in countries with low levels of inequality (Japan, the Netherlands, Scandinavian countries), compared with countries with high levels of inequality such as the US, South Africa and the UK.

Countries with low levels of inequality have higher than average life expectancies and contribute more to international aid as a percentage of GDP. The percentage is highest in Scandinavian countries (0.8–1.0%) and lowest in the US and Australia (around 0.2%), which are also leaders in inequality.

Mutual trust is an important factor in ensuring that a society functions effectively. Absence of trust leads to heightened anxiety, insecurity, violence, isolation and mental ill-health. Trust boosts cooperation and is closely linked to levels of equality. Levels of trust in the US have fallen from 60% in 1960 to 40% by 2004, corresponding to increased levels of inequality (NORC, 2004).

Inequality leads to stigmatisation where 'sub' groups within society are blamed for their lack of income and opportunity. Conversely, solidarity benefits the poor but it also benefits middle and wealthy classes who fare better with reduced disparity. The evidence consistently shows that growth is more persistent in more equal countries and, throughout this period of growth, income distribution is the most significant factor (Berg, 2012).

The evidence decimates the arguments rolled out by American conservatives who consistently state that too much equalisation stifles growth. This hypothesis suggests that the rich getting richer stimulates the economy and benefits everyone. In fact, the evidence shows that the opposite is true – the poor getting richer benefits everyone, including the rich (Wilkinson & Pichett, 2010).

In terms of reducing inequality, the first step is to revise downwards the debts of poor countries and provide, at a feasible price, renewable energy sources, basic healthcare and food, if required. Food self-sufficiency is essential, as well as methods of economic regulation that check artificial fluctuations in the price of staple goods, which are essentially the causes of economic collapse for small producers. Systems of transparency and accountability are also essential (Morin, 2014).

Morin and Hesel (2014) also proposes the creation, at an international level, of a 'permanent council' to fight inequality which would have the dual role of monitoring the causes of inequality, as well as finding remedies to reduce inequality.

In Scandinavian countries, a major source of equality is the redistribution of state resources. Taxation is high and social services are comprehensive, allowing adequate provision for the underprivileged. This has not prevented Scandinavia from being one of the most stable regions in the world with consistently high levels of growth.

Other proposals to reduce inequality include the following (Ricard, 2013):

- Clamping down on corruption, nepotism and lobbying – all of which allow those in positions of power to exercise pressure on governments to enjoy monopolies that allow them to maintain a stranglehold on the markets. Banks and big businesses put pressure on the state at times of crises under the pretext that they are too big to fail.

- Reducing exploitation and wastage and establishing effective social welfare systems that provide for the poorest and the youngest.

- Income tax and wealth tax must be seen as a way of financing the state and reducing inequality. With this in mind, tax systems must be seen as fair and efficient and tax havens abolished.

- The underprivileged need increased access to healthcare, education and training – this constitutes long-term social investment. Evidence from the OECD confirms that, contrary to popular opinion, tackling inequalities through taxation and other redistribution policies does not harm growth, provided these policies are well designed and implemented (OECD, 2014).

Social Business

It is possible to have an economic and political system that has equity as a fundamental core value with the well-being of all its citizens and respect for the environment as key principals underpinning all policy, including policy directed at economic growth.

The reality is that the free market does not work as well as its supporters claim. Instead of leading to greater stability, recent global market crashes show this to be untrue. Invariably, following a market crash, many working in the financial sector walk away with substantial bonuses, while those who suffered as a result of the crisis often lose their jobs. Wealth accrued by the elite arises out of their ability to take advantage of others.

Efforts to curb exorbitant pay and bonuses have been shown to be effective. Switzerland has introduced a policy that curbs 'excessive pay packages' for company bosses as well as making incentive bonuses to join a company and golden handshakes illegal.

Altruism by its nature is contagious and plays a positive and important role in society. The opposite is also true. Selfishness breeds selfishness – the policies of US President Donald Trump's Republican Party are testament to that. In fact, there is a body of evidence that suggests reciprocity results in a more efficient and productive economy. It promotes efficiency and transparency, because information is shared rather than monopolised or concealed, as happens in most big companies. Altruistic motivations promote cooperation which boosts productivity and increases fairness in the production and distribution of resources, as well as reducing spending normally apportioned to competition. It also improves working relations and creativity.

Muhammad Yunus, speaking at the World Economic Forum in Davos, 2010, during a session on 'Rethinking Values in a Post-Crisis World' said the following:

> We do not need to change the way business is done, we simply need to change its goals. There is selfish business the purpose

> of which is just profit for a few people. It reduces humanity to a single dimension, money, and thus ignores our humanity. Then there is selfless business, the goal of which is primarily, to serve society. This is also known as social business. Charity is a one-time giving that can be very helpful but it does not have sustainable effects. Social business can help society in a sustainable way (Ricard, 2013).

Social business is viable and can be profitable. But the direct beneficiary is society. The business may create jobs or provide a product – these are its direct goals, not making money for the sake of it. Some countries have taken on this social and solidarity based economy more than others.

This is a move away from the single thinking that is the markets, instead favouring mutual assistance that places the principals of social justice and equal opportunities at its core. These are the principals on which fair trade and ethical funds are based.

These initiatives which dispel traditional economic teaching and systems are based around cooperation, openness and trust and ultimately work better.

Voluntary Simplicity

Gandhi is quoted as defining civilisation as follows: 'Civilisation, in the real sense of the term, consists not in the multiplication but in the deliberate and voluntary reduction of wants. This alone promotes real happiness and contentment, and increases the capacity for service' (Gandhi, 2008).

This 'voluntary reduction' does not involve depriving us of what makes us happy but coming to a better understanding of how to achieve genuine satisfaction and to stop being addicted to consumer items which are, in many ways, the cause of unhappiness.

'Voluntary simplicity' is a different concept. Rather than depriving us of what makes us happy, it involves reaching a better understanding of how to achieve satisfaction and to curb the addiction to consumerist pleasures which are the basis of our suffering. Voluntary simplicity is rather the basis of a more lasting contentment.

Voluntary simplicity has been described as being 'outwardly simple, inwardly rich'. It involves examining what is usually regarded as being indispensable and checking whether it genuinely improves our well-being. It involves living a simpler life, centring and what is genuine and indispensable and extracting the material benefits that are accompanied by high stress levels. It focuses on the power of 'happy moderation' – deciding to curb materialism and return humanity to the forefront of our preoccupations. Living in larger and more stylish homes, travelling frequently and eating sophisticated food comes with a cost; consuming time, energy, attention and ultimately, well-being. Voluntary simplicity removes you from the vicious cycle of constantly needing more, as well as reducing the gap between rich and poor.

During the 2008 financial crisis in the US, George W. Bush urged American citizens to start consuming as much as possible; the logic being that the more that was consumed the faster the economy would recover and the happier people would be. This logic does not correspond with scientific research. Studies spanning several decades and samples of thousands of participants from across the entire population, have established that consumer societies are overall less satisfied with their lives than those who focus on more fundamental values in life, such as friendship, happiness, quality of life experiences and concern for others, as well as responsibility towards society and the environment (Kasser, 2003).

Consumers tend to have fewer positive emotions – experiencing less joy, enthusiasm and gratitude than those less preoccupied by consumer culture. They experience more anxiety and depression and are more subject to physical symptoms such as headaches and stomach pain. They have less vitality and consume more addictive substances such as alcohol and cigarettes, as well as watching more television. Feelings of depression are more likely to be addressed by further consumption.

These studies also show that materialists show below average levels of empathy and compassion towards those who are suffering and tend to exploit others to their advantage. They prefer competition to cooperation and have little concern with the environment. Social ties are weaker, friendships are more superficial and less longstanding than the rest of the population (Kasser, 2003).

This negative correlation between consumerist tendencies and well-being has been observed in a wide variety of settings across North and South America, as well as Europe and Asia. In summary, the research shows that a preference for consumption and materialism forms an obstacle to the establishment of caring and harmonious human interactions. Furthermore, achieving goals linked to humane values leads to greater levels of satisfaction than the realisation of material objectives (Rockström, 2009).

Research also shows that once a threshold of material comfort is achieved, increasing wealth does not lead to a corresponding increase in quality of life (Myers, 2000). Western cultures with excessive levels of consumer goods, as well as high-quality jobs and better healthcare, are not happier than cultures with far less. There are many other factors more important than wealth.

Trust is one. Denmark has been identified as a country where people are most satisfied with their living conditions. Despite being less wealthy than many other western cultures, it has very little poverty and inequality. What has been gauged is a high level of trust that people feel toward each other, including towards strangers and institutions. This trust goes hand in hand with low levels of corruption.

High levels of wealth correlates with personal satisfaction when that wealth is spent on others to improve their well-being. This phenomenon has been identified with large scale philanthropy as well as in small donations (Dunn, 2008).

There is therefore poor correlation between money and happiness. Researchers suggest that in order to find happiness, compulsive consumers would be better off pursuing experiences rather than material goods, as well as using their money to benefit others rather than themselves and paying close attention to the happiness of others (Dunn, 2011).

If we want to live in a flourishing, equitable and sustainable society, we need to focus on the concepts of altruism and cooperation as a way of achieving economic sustainability, as well as physical and mental well-being, both for ourselves and for the generations that will follow.

Catherine Conlon is director of health and nutrition at Safefood, the all-island organisation that provides advice on food safety, healthy eating and food hygiene for consumers.

References

Berg, A., Ostry, J.D., Zettelmeyer, J. (2012). 'What Makes Growth Sustained?'. *Journal of Economic Development*, 98(2):149–166.

Dunn, E. (2008). 'Spending Money on Others Promotes Happiness'. *Science*, 319(5870):1687.

Dunn, D. (2011). 'If Money Doesn't Make You Happy, Then You Probably Aren't Spending It Right'. *Journal of Consumer Psychology*, 21(2), 115.
Harari, Y.N. (2018). *21 lessons for the 21st Century*. Spiegel and Grau.
Johnson, D.W., & Johnson, R.T. (1999). 'Making Cooperative Learning Work'. *Theory into Practice*, 38:67–73.
Kasser, T. (2003). *The High Price of Materialism*. Cambridge, Mass.: MIT.
Morin, E., & Hessel, S. (2014). *The Path to Hope*. New York: Other Press.
Myer, D. (2000). 'The Funds, Faith and Friends of Happy People'. *American Psychologist*, 55(1):56.
National Organisation for Research and Computing. (2004). *Annual Report 2004*.
Neapolitan, J. (1999). 'A Comparative Analysis of Nations with Low and High Levels of Violent Crime'. *Journal of Criminal Justice*, 27(3), 259–274.
OECD. (2019). *Inequality – Poverty Rate – OECD Data*. Available at: https://data.oecd.org/inequality/poverty-rate.htm
Plety, R. (1996). *Cooperative Learning*. Lyons: Lyons University.
Ricard, M.R. (2013). *Altruism: The Science and Psychology of Kindness*. New York: Little, Brown and Company.
Rockström, J. (2009). 'A Safe Operating Space for Humanity'. *Nature*, 461(7263), 472–475.
Seligman, M. (2011). *Flourish: A Visionary New Understanding of Health and Well-being*. New York, Free Press.
Wilkinson, R., & Pickett, K. (2010). *The Spirit Level*. London: Penguin.
Wolff, E.N. (2017). *Household Wealth Trends in the United States, 1962 to 2016: Has Middle Class Wealth Recovered?*. Working Paper 24085. Cambridge, MA: NBER.

SELFISHNESS AND ALTRUISM

WILLIAM O'HALLORAN

Personal Journey

I went to a five-year-old's birthday party recently with my soon-to-be four-year-old daughter. She's a very inquisitive young lady and I found myself having to explain why it's not such a good thing for people to get so many presents and to own so many things. In a typical child's eyes, there's nothing that could be more wonderful than to be showered with well over twenty gifts on a single occasion. To an adult with a better understanding of the concept of materialistic consumer culture, such an amount of gifts should seem excessive. So, the question was, why is it bad to get so many presents? The simple answer I gave was based on trees and forests. I explained that in order to make presents, trees need to be cut down and that it is okay to cut down trees from time to time. The problem is that when we decide that we need so many presents, then entire forests have to be cut down. I was happy with my explanation and so was my daughter. She could understand why we wouldn't want to cut down whole forests because she likes forests. She knows that they are more fun to play in than playing can be with any of her toys. To not buy presents for our daughter would be mean and the point I'm making is certainly not about parents being ungenerous to their kids. Instead, the point is that the birthday party was a metaphor for what's wrong with society in Ireland and in the world in general. Too many of us see no problem with ignoring the impacts our overly excessive consumer lifestyles are having on the rest of nature. Our selfish attitude and ignorance is not serving the natural world and, in turn, it is not serving us.

We rely on biodiversity for almost every aspect of our well-being, yet 'around the world, the library of life that has evolved over billions of years – our biodiversity – is being destroyed, poisoned, polluted, invaded, fragmented, plundered, drained and burned at a rate not seen in human history' (Higgins, 2019). The year 2019 brought us the first National Biodiversity conference in Ireland and those who attended were provided with a snapshot of the health of the Irish landscape and all who live in it. As one would expect, there were a lot of positive stories about people working together to do what they can for nature, but the overarching theme from the event was that we need to be doing more than we have been doing thus far.

We need biodiversity to provide us with clean air, water, food, fuel and medicines. We also avail of biodiversity services in terms of recreation and spiritual enrichment. It plays a crucial role in supporting pollination and soil fertility, and protecting us from extreme weather and the threats associated with environmental issues such as climate change (NPWS, 2017). For well over a decade, climate change has been considered the most serious environmental issue that human societies have ever faced (O'Brien, St. Clair, & Kristofferson, 2010).

I have always had a deep sense of care and affection towards the natural world and though I can point to many reasons, I can't really say why. My life experience and interaction with nature from an early age has been important in shaping how I feel about nature, but I believe there's something more primal at play. I can remember my mother driving me to school one day when I was around seven years old. As we travelled, I saw across the valley an area of scrubby woodland the size of a football field being destroyed by large machinery. I implored my mother to find out why this was happening and to see if something could be done to rescue the wood. To her credit, she spoke to the landowners and they told her that they were simply cleaning up the land and that they were going to plant new trees in place of the old ones. Though this was not a good thing to be doing from an ecological perspective, with my own level of understanding at the time I was satisfied to hear the news. Since that time, I have encountered many other people who feel the same way about nature.

I work on the Wild Work initiative for a local development company called SECAD Partnership in Co. Cork. I am lucky to interact with a diverse range of people across society, all with an interest in helping nature – people in local communities of all ages, people in industry, people in state agencies and people in academia. With Wild Work, we help people, to help nature, to help people. We connect people together to help make positive actions happen on the ground. The work we do is complimentary to a range of regional and national plans and policies related to human health and biodiversity. Our focus is on bringing wildness back into people's lives; because nature needs us, but not as much as we need nature.

On Friday, 15 March 2019, in Ireland and throughout the world young people stood together to say that the time for talk on climate change has past and now is the time for action. Their message was that without action, there is no hope. I didn't get to go to the strike, but I did pour over news footage from the day's events. Though I don't often cry, I shed tears that night with a little sense of sadness for this world, but more so with an overwhelming sense of pride for what I was witnessing. I sensed real power among people who have decided we must derail the destructive train of modern society; a society that has lived so inconsiderately with regard to its impact on our natural world. Hopefully the young people will have an impact. To me, they already have. I am thirty-five years old. Most of these powerful people are not even adults.

Protesting is important, but I guess it's not my thing. I haven't been at a protest since my early twenties. Some time ago I decided that I would focus my efforts on sharing the wonder of nature with people. Spreading the gospel of nature with the hope that one day we will have enough people who care about making a difference for nature, because I believe that is the biggest way in which we can make a difference in this world. Connecting people with nature has always been what I've considered my work. It's important work that I believe makes a difference because helping people to develop their own sense of understanding and care towards the natural world should help them stand up for it when the need arises. The climate strike gave me a sense of achievement. The nature educators of this world are beginning to make a difference. That's what I felt.

Climate change and biodiversity loss are serious environmental issues. They can be deeply saddening for people who contemplate and try to understand their associated impacts. With climate change we are presented with a scenario that isn't going to end well for any of us, unless we radically change our ways. Some people say it isn't an issue at all. However, it's fair to say that the general consensus is that the negative scenario is the more likely. These issues should not be ignored, yet largely they have been. Biodiversity loss, in my opinion, is an even more serious issue than climate change. Many people would consider that both issues are one and the same thing and in ways they are. From what I've seen this year, I'm glad that Ireland is reaching an age of awareness on both issues. The enthusiasm is there to make a difference.

State of the Irish Environment

An analysis carried out by Irish environmental NGOs found that Ireland is performing unsatisfactorily in terms of management of protected sites, species protection, enhancing landscape connectivity for wildlife, preventing the escalation of issues associated with non-native species, stakeholder engagement, public participation and communication (Birdlife International, 2018).

In terms of species and habitats in Ireland that are considered threatened across Europe and protected under the Habitats Directive, 52% of species are in favourable status. This might sound like an acceptable percentage, but there are ominous signs for the future survival of our wildlife species when you consider that only 9% of habitats are in favourable status (NPWS, 2013).

Our Natural Origins

The plants and animals living in Ireland today have arrived here as a result of a most complex sequence of survival and migration associated with ice-age advancement and retreat, the sea-level changes this led to and other factors such as human influence. There is a lot still to be learned about our flora and fauna, and an ongoing debate about which species are natives and which are not. Prior to the Stone Age or Neolithic period, we know little about the few thousand years of ice-free Ireland in terms of its history of human inhabitancy. It was once thought that all of our flora and fauna species migrated across a land bridge between Ireland and Britain as sea levels changed. However, over time we have discovered linkages between Ireland and the Iberian Peninsula and have learned of species such as the Kerry slug found only in both places, telling us a story of an interlinked past (Cabot, 1999).

As mentioned, evidence has not yet been found for human settlement in Ireland during the Palaeolithic, or 'Early Stone Age' period. This is almost unique in Europe and creates a sense of intrigue as to who the first people to live on Irish shores were (O'Brien, 2012). As the Ice Age drew to a close, around ten thousand years ago, vegetation communities developed successionally, with grassland habitats and scrub being superseded by a deciduous woodland climax phase which saw the finest years of Ireland's woodlands lasting between five thousand and seven thousand years. This climax phase was dominated by tree species such as hazel, oak, elm and alder and supported impressive fauna such as wolves and bears (Cabot, 1999). It gives a great sense of wonder to imagine that unspoilt wilderness first lived in by Irish hunter-gatherers and then by the earliest of Irish Stone Age farmers. What remains of biodiversity in the Irish landscape today is like a skeleton from that past. We have stripped our landscape back to the bare bones. That may sound dark and depressing, but looking on the brighter side, the reality is that all is not destroyed. We do still have wonderful natural places in Ireland today and amazing wildlife throughout our urban and rural landscape. We can put meat back on the bones.

Though not a typical exercise, I took a look at detailed aerial imagery of modern-day Ireland and came to the conclusion that about 25% of our landscape is in a healthy state with regard to biodiversity. That's not to say that the remaining 75% is destroyed and it's important to acknowledge that it also depends on how you define a healthy state. For those interested, looking at aerial imagery of Ireland and trying to interpret the percentage of what you might define as 'healthy landscape' is an exercise worth doing sometime. On the positive side, you can drop a pin anywhere on a map of Ireland and travel to that place and be guaranteed of finding something of biodiversity importance within a kilometre or less. You can't say the same for other parts of the world.

Changes in the Agricultural Landscape

The long history of human influence in Europe has meant that most landscapes are highly modified and that most ecosystems lie along a scale between artificial and what's called 'semi-natural' (Perrow & Davy, 2002). Farming has shaped almost all parts of the landscape. Considering our past and the importance of food for human survival, citizens of Ireland should have a considerable interest in the overall health of our agricultural industry. Though we have evolved in recent years, we were once largely an agrarian society. My own family situation is testament to big changes that have occurred in Irish farming with regards to people moving away from the land. My four grandparents all grew up on farms or food growing holdings, but today not a single one of their grandchildren is making a living from farming the land. As the oldest grandchild, I was lucky that they shared some of their knowledge and that they taught me important lessons about the way of life from their childhoods and about the life skills people had in their communities. Passed down through generations, we had fully natural and sustainable community-based farming systems throughout Ireland that were largely self-sufficient.

Changes in agricultural practices gathered pace in Ireland in the 1900s. The mechanisation of farming, demands for mass production resulting from food shortages associated with wars and the development of the practice of 'improvement' were important factors (Jonathan & Watson, 2008). Irish farming systems moved away from self-sufficient models towards models of increased inputs, outputs and mass production. This contributed to drastic landscape change and wildlife loss. For example, we got rid of the majority of our semi-natural grasslands and replaced them with monocultures of ryegrass crops better suited to intensive farming. Though there are many impressive aspects of modern Irish farming, in changing our agricultural landscape we lost things that we took for granted. The hay meadows of older self-sufficient systems contained great floral diversity. Some plant species were of particular importance to the health of animals. Plantains and buttercups contain one hundred and sixty times the concentration of cobalt as grasses, while dandelion nettles and thistles have up to five times the proportion of copper as grasses (Mabey, 2010).

Growing only the same crop or keeping just the one type of animal on the same plot of land is not the natural order of things (Seymour, 2003). As one thing has led to another, we now have farming systems in Ireland that can no longer be described as self-sufficient. The pig as an animal almost seems designed with self-sufficiency in mind. It is perhaps the most omnivorous animal in the world and can convert almost anything produced on a farm into meat. It can also improve land for cultivation purposes (Seymour, 2003). Pigs are especially useful in that they can turn surplus quantities of food in productive times of the year into meat that can be availed of in leaner times of year. Pigs aren't raised on scraps anymore. While the nation eats lots of pigs and turns a blind eye to any of the issues, the pig has undergone a transformation in terms of its role and how it is treated today. What was once the ultimate free-ranging sustainability animal on Irish farms and a crucially important part of the self-sufficient farmstead is now mass produced indoors in a less ethical and less environmentally friendly way (Pig Industry Stakeholder Group, 2016).

As a nation, if we reflect on our agricultural system from pre-EU times, then it's fair to say that we had a more self-sufficient model in terms of feeding local communities and the country as a whole. Feeding the planet is a different matter. I have often heard that the need for mass production in Ireland's agricultural sector is based on the demands we face in terms of feeding the planet. I would suggest that the bigger factor is a desire to feed our economy.

Connection with Nature

It is theorised that an enhanced sense of connection with the natural world inspires empathy that in turn leads to pro-environmental behaviour (Britain, Elise, & Manning, 2014). However, there are people who view humans as nothing more than destructive beings that care little for other species of life. That might not be a fair way of judging us as a species. Have you ever come across an animal in need of rescue, such as a rabbit that's been knocked down by a car? In such scenarios, not everyone would bother to help the unfortunate animal, but lots of people would. Walk through a supermarket and you'll find shelves stocked with food for wild birds. It has been argued that our natural affinity for life binds us to all other living species and that this love of life is the essence of our humanity, rooted deep in our ancestral past (Wilson, 1984). This human love of all that is alive is known as 'biophilia' (Fromm, 1974). The idea that humans innately care about nature is something that sets us apart from other species and it is an important thing to consider when looking for solutions towards a more sustainable future. By tapping into people's innate love of other species of life, it can become easier to convince people to act to help nature here in Ireland.

Spending time in nature affects how we think about nature. It has been shown that people who have regular interactions with wild ecosystems are more likely to make pro-environmental choices (Britain, Elise, & Manning, 2014). Henry David Thoreau, the nineteenth century writer and philosopher, taught us that if people refuse to play by the rules of hard work and wealth accumulation, the rules of a nation governed by a consumerist and competitive mentality, then we can gain the freedom to adapt to the natural world around us and live a simpler, more enjoyable life (Thoreau, 1997).

William O'Halloran is a team leader at Wild Work, a unique initiative with biodiversity at its heart. Wild Work is committed to helping nature and its particular focus is to connect business, biodiversity and local communities. It also supports the work of both local and national organisations involved in the conservation and protection of the natural environment.

References

Birdlife International. (2018). *The State of Implementation of the Birds and Habitats Directives in the EU: An analysis by national environmental NGOs in 18 member states*. Europe: Birdlife Interantional, European Environment Bureau, Friends of the Earth Europe, World Wildlife Federation.

Britain, S.A., Elise, A.L., & Manning, C.M. (2014). 'In and Of the Wilderness: Ecological Connection Through Participation in Nature'. *Ecopsychology*, 6(2), 81–90.

Cabot, D. (1999). *Ireland*. London: Harper Collins Publishers.

Fromm, E. (1974). *The Anatomy of Human Destructiveness*. London: Random House.

Higgins, M.D. (2019). *New Horizons for Nature: National Biodiversity Conference*. Dublin: President of Ireland. Retrieved 25 March 2019, from: https://president.ie/en/diary/details/president-addresses-the-national-biodiversityconference/speeches

Jonathan, B., & Watson, M. (2008). *A History of Irish Farming 1750–1950*. Dublin: Four Courts Press.

Mabey, R. (2010). *Weeds: How Vagabond Plants Gatecrashed Civilization and Changed the Way We Think About Nature*. London: Profile Books Ltd.

NPWS. (2013). *The Status of EU Protected Habitats and Species in Ireland 2013 – Overview Volume 1 – Unpublished report, National Parks and Wildlife Service*. Dublin: Dept. of Arts, Heritage and the Gaeltacht. Retrieved 5 February 2019, from: https://www.npws.ie/sites/default/files/publications/pdf/Art17-Vol1-web.pdf

NPWS. (2017). *National Biodiversity Plan 2017–2021*. Dublin: Dept. of Culture, Heritage and the Gaeltacht. Retrieved 5 February 2019, from: https://www.npws.ie/sites/default/files/publications/pdf/National%20Biodiversity%20Action%20Plan%20English.pdf

O'Brien, K., St. Clair, A.L., & Kristofferson, B. (2010). *Climate Change, Ethics and Human Security*. Cambridge: Cambridge University Press.

O'Brien, W. (2012). *Iverni: A Prehistory of Cork*. Cork: The Collins Press.

Perrow, M.R., & Davy, A.J. (2002). *Handbook of Ecological Restoration: Restoration in Practice*, vol. 2. Cambridge: Cambridge University Press.

Pig Industry Stakeholder Group. (2016). *Report of the Pig Industry Stakeholder Group*. Ireland: Pig Industry Stakeholder Group. Retrieved 9 April 2019, from: https://www.agriculture.gov.ie/media/migration/farmingsectors/pigs/REPORTPIGINDUSTSTAKEHOLDERGROUP290116.pdf

Seymour, J. (2003). *The New Complete Book of Self-Sufficiency: The Classic Guide for Realists and Dreamers*. London: Dorling Kindersley.

Thoreau, H.D. (1997). *Walden*. Oxford: Oxford University Press.

Wilson, E.O. (1984). *Biophilia*. Cambridge: Harvard University Presss.

SURFING THE WAVES OF CHANGE: STRENGTHENING LOCAL RESILIENCE IN A CHANGING SOCIETY

DAVIE PHILIP

Planet Earth is in jeopardy. Globally we have entered into an era of rising temperatures, species extinction, water shortages, wildfires, extreme weather, conflict and mass migration. Locally our communities are fragmented, vulnerable and already suffering from an epidemic of loneliness. We now need to collectively redesign how we live on this planet, moving away from a culture that is predominantly degenerative to one that is regenerative. An agenda of deep adaptation is now required if we are to respond to the climate emergency. Are we up for the task ahead?

Over the next thirty years we are likely to see more change and disturbance than at any other period in recorded human history. So how do we cope with these converging challenges, and at the same time, accelerate a transition towards a future that is more sustainable, just and resilient?

With the possibility of abrupt breakdowns in our vital social, economic and environmental systems becoming more likely if we don't take action, we have to find ways in which every community and every citizen can play a part in the transition. An unprecedented mobilisation of people and resources is essential to secure the well-being and resilience of our societies and prevent the worst of climate breakdown. Can we surf these waves of change?

The alarm bells have been ringing unheeded for a long time and governments have been talking about ensuring a sustainable planet for decades. In 1992, at the first the Earth Summit in Rio de Janeiro, world leaders listened to the warnings and agreed on the need for the integration of economic development, environmental protection and social justice. In 2000, the Millennium Summit in New York resulted in the Millennium Development Goals, eight targets for developing countries to be reached by the year 2015. In 2012, twenty years after the first Earth Summit at an event to mark the occasion, the UN published *The Future We Want*, which committed to develop the Sustainable Development Goals, a blueprint to achieve a better and more sustainable future for all.

The year 2015 was a significant one for international agreements. Ireland, along with one hundred and ninety-two other countries, signed up to adopt the 2030 Agenda for Sustainable Development and committed to the seventeen Sustainable Development Goals (SDGs). This is a mechanism to mobilise efforts to end poverty, protect the planet and ensure prosperity for everyone. The SDGs are nothing new; however, they do give us a common framework and language to discuss and act on the issues across sectors.

Also that year, the UN Framework Convention on Climate Change (UNFCCC) adopted the Paris Agreement, a legally-binding framework for an internationally coordinated effort to tackle climate change. One hundred and ninety-five nations agreed to adopt green energy sources, cut greenhouse gas emissions and limit the rise of global temperatures to below 2°C above pre-industrial times and 'endeavour to limit' them even more, to 1.5°C. This agreement brings (almost) all nations into a common cause to undertake ambitious efforts to combat climate change and adapt to its effects. Enhanced support is promised to assist developing countries and the people who have contributed the least to the crisis but who are going to be affected most.

It is hard to be optimistic that these goals and targets will be achieved. Implementation will be hindered by existing power structures and inherently unsustainable and inequitable economic models. We currently lack the required political will, policy coherence and means of cooperation to deliver them. All the blame for inaction can't be directed at politicians, the majority of citizens are oblivious to the severity of these issues and are not taking or demanding action. There are, however, some hopeful signs that we are waking up to the scale of the challenge.

Millions of students all across the planet have been walking out of school every Friday for a liveable future. A climate emergency is being declared by town councils and local authorities across the UK, and, in the US, individual states are committing to plans genuinely in line with meeting climate targets. A 'Green New Deal' to address both the financial and environmental crises, inspired by the New Deal programmes that helped the US get out of the Great Depression of the 1930s, is being called for by progressive politicians. This will make unprecedented investment in clean energy, warm homes, affordable public transport, sustainable farming, and restored natural habitats – delivering much-needed jobs and livelihoods.

A movement of community-led and cooperative initiatives are emerging across the world that are pioneering change at the local level. These include community energy initiatives, cooperative banks, micro credit schemes, ecovillages, co-housing neighbourhoods, co-working spaces, car clubs, digital fabrication labs and community-supported agriculture projects. Based on ecological and human values, these social innovations are building community and transforming local economies. They are innovating new ways of doing, thinking and organising, and are challenging the dominant narrative of extreme competition and individualism.

These pioneers are still outliers, operating on the margins of society and well below the radar of policymakers and mainstream media, but are demonstrating that democracy and economic life can be radically reorganised from the bottom up. They highlight values of altruism, empathy and solidarity, and practices such as sharing, collective ownership and local resilience. They counter the widespread loss of connection between ourselves and our environment, while at the same time nurturing social relationships, creating livelihoods and developing more sustainable communities.

The International Panel on Climate Change issued a stark warning in 2018, the Earth is warming faster than previously predicted and we have only a twelve-year window to make rapid changes or face a largely uninhabitable planet by the end of this century. Climate is already forcing entire communities from their homes across the globe. Weather incidents are becoming more severe, even here in

Ireland. Whatever we do we are now locked into disruptions that we are completely unprepared for.

A focus needs to be on local resilience, how communities might cope in uncertain times. Building resilience can help localities develop the ability to face challenges in ways that strengthen their social bonds, better steward resources, enhance our capacity to deal with change and allow us to spring forward from adversity strengthened and more resourceful. This transformational view of resilience emphasises renewal, regeneration and re-organisation, it is not just about recovering or preparing for shock.

If we are to really adapt to the challenges we face today and navigate the uncertainty ahead, we will need to nurture greater collaboration within and across different sectors. There is a massive opportunity now for building new coalitions and social enterprises that can creatively transform the way we do almost everything.

As well as strengthening the resilience of our communities and transforming the way we meet our needs, a fundamental change in the way we think is also necessary. As the business educator Peter Drucker stressed: 'the greatest danger in times of turbulence is not the turbulence – it is to act with yesterday's logic.' Similarly, Albert Einstein famously said, 'No problem can be solved from the same level of consciousness that created it.' To make the transition to a healthy society based on fairness, well-being and sustainability, we need to shift our worldview and open our minds and hearts to fresh ways of thinking.

Currently, we are locked into an individualistic worldview where reductionist or mechanistic thinking dominates. This mindset breaks everything down into parts to be analysed and measured. By understanding the parts and how they function, we presume we can understand everything important there is to know about something. This reductionism is very useful for understanding inanimate things, or simple systems like machines, but can be problematic when applied to living systems.

The world is complex and to thrive in it we need a transformation from an outdated 'ego-system' mindset, focused on the well-being of oneself, to an 'eco-system' awareness which emphasises the health of the whole. Holism or systems-thinking can help do this. In this worldview, complex systems are not understood by breaking them apart, but by focusing on the relationships between the parts and within the context of larger systems.

More joined-up thinking is needed to achieve a sustainable future. We need to think relationally. The interconnectedness between all forms of life is recognised with systems-thinking. A holistic mindset is conducive to being adaptive and tends to value caring, empathy and cooperation. Reductionist thinkers have a tendency to hold a fixed way of seeing the world and value wealth, power, prestige and fame. Another assumption underlying the dominant reductionist worldview is the dualistic separation between us and nature.

We justify our superiority over the environment when we think we are separate and with this worldview we create fragile, linear systems. Through the diversity and complexity of their webs of relationships, and by sharing resources across their boundaries, living systems increase well-being and resilience. Observing these patterns and principles of natural systems might provide us with vital insights into how to redesign our socio-economic systems to be collaborative, regenerative and resilient.

Climate change, soil loss, species extinction, social breakdown, inequality and all the other issues we urgently need to respond to are all symptoms of the way we live and use resources. Probably our biggest global challenge right now is our inability to imagine a society not based on extraction and exploitation. As we wake up to the existential threat faced we need to adopt and scale up the many regenerative and resilient initiatives that have been prototyped at the margins of society. This could be a driving force for making sustainability a reality in our local communities.

These new stories of communities taking control and reimagining the future need to be accessible and applicable for more people. In his book *Out of the Wreckage,* George Monbiot suggests that, 'it is through restoring community, renewing civic life and claiming our place in the world, we build a society in which our extraordinary nature – our altruism, empathy and deep connection – is released.'

We are truly living in interesting times. No one can predict the future but what is certain is that we have entered a storm that shows no sign of ending any time soon. The present challenges do provide an opportunity for refocusing how we want to live. Coming together across sectorial, national and ideological divides to collaborate in implementing the SDGs and climate targets is important.

We have to start in our own cities, neighbourhoods, villages, organisations and in our own lives. By reconnecting with each other and the natural world around us we could fulfil our own material, spiritual and emotional needs in a way that is in balance with the needs of society and that don't undermine our life-support systems. By cultivating community and nurturing our resilience we can surf the powerful waves of change ahead.

Davie Philip is a facilitator and trainer with the Sustainable Ireland Cooperative who trade as Cultivate (www.cultivate.ie). He designs and delivers networking and learning events including the annual Convergence sustainable living festival. Davie was a founding member of both FEASTA: the Foundation for the Economics of Sustainability and Sustainable Projects Ireland, the company behind the ecovillage project in Cloughjordan, Co. Tipperary where he is now based.

SECTION SIX

THE WAY FORWARD

Sustainable development is the pathway to the future we want for all. It offers a framework to generate economic growth, achieve social justice, exercise environmental stewardship and strengthen governance.

Ban Ki-moon

IMPACT OF MODERN CULTURE ON BIODIVERSITY

LIAM LYSAGHT

Emergence of Biodiversity as a Concept

Biodiversity is a modern term used to describe the variety of life on this planet. It differs from the more traditional term 'nature' in that biodiversity acknowledges that human activity is an integral part of, rather than external to, the natural world; and efforts to conserve biodiversity must incorporate human activity. Tracking the evolution of approaches to nature conservation over the last century sheds some light on how culture and biodiversity are intertwined. Traditionally, the hunting and exploitation of animals was considered the biggest threat to biodiversity and the earliest laws reflected this. In Ireland, the Wildlife Act of 1976, the central plank of national nature conservation legislation, placed a significant emphasis on controlling and licensing the impact of hunting. The Act also sought to provide legal protection to the best wildlife sites in the country. By the time of the Convention on Biological Diversity in 1990, there was a realisation that the conservation of biological diversity could not be achieved through protecting sites alone, but that conservation also had to be achieved in the wider countryside and that all sectors of society had a role to play.

More recently, the concept of 'ecosystem services' is being promoted. This argues for the conservation of nature from a more utilitarian perspective, stressing the value of the ecological processes and services that we take for granted including water purification, productive soils, climate regulation, carbon sequestration, pollination, pest control, all of which bring enormous benefits to Irish society and the economy. The assumption is that if the monetary value of the ecosystem goods and services are quantified and built into more broadly based accountancy systems, then there is a greater likelihood that society will place more value in conserving these services.

The Changing Biodiversity Landscape

In Ireland, only a few lonely voices raised concerns about the human impacts on nature during the early decades of the twentieth century. However, by the 1960s conservation was becoming an increasing concern, largely driven by evidence of the impact arterial draining programmes, pollution and excessive shooting pressure was having on wetland bird populations. This led to the formation of the Irish Wildbird Conservancy, which remains to this day, probably the most influential NGOs for nature conservation in this country.

Ireland's entry into the European Economic Community (EEC) in 1973, and the Common Agricultural Policy was to have a profound impact on the pace and scale of management of the Irish landscape, and consequently Ireland's biodiversity. The combination of a modernising Ireland, greater availability of cash through direct payments, easier access to machinery for land management, and a headlong drive for a 'maximising production' model of agriculture meant nature and biodiversity were increasingly driven to the margins. This trend has continued unabated until the present day.

The Evidence for Our Biodiversity Crisis

There is ever increasing evidence that biodiversity is in serious trouble. Recently two new synthesis reports have highlighted the seriousness of the situation. Towards the end of 2018, the World Wildlife Fund for Nature published its Living Planet Report for 2018 (WWF, 2018), which reports on its Living Planet Index. The Living Planet Index is 'an indicator of the state of global biodiversity and the health of our planet and it tracks the population abundance of thousands of mammals, birds, fish, reptiles and amphibians from around the world'. Based on this index it found that there has been an astonishingly steep fall of 60% in biodiversity over the last forty years.

Earlier this year, a review of seventy-three insects studies from across the world (Sánchez-Bayo & Wyckhuys, 2019) showed that insect populations were experiencing an alarming decline of 2.5% per annum, and that more than 40% of insect species are declining. Alarming as this study is, results from the Irish Bumblebee Monitoring Scheme and the Irish Butterfly Monitoring Schemes both managed by the National Biodiversity Data Centre, showed an even larger year-on-year decline in these groups of insects in Ireland; here butterflies have declined by 2.6% over the last ten years, whereas bumblebee populations have declined by a shocking 3.7% over the last six years.

These findings reflect a pattern which is evident across different groups of organisms in Ireland. Of the thousand or so species that have undergone a formal conservation assessment in Ireland, on average about one in four species is threatened with extinction here. Threatened species include familiar species such as Atlantic salmon, European eel, curlew, hen harrier, yellowhammer, freshwater pearl mussel and angel shark. This is a truly shocking legacy that we are handing on to future generations. The most succinct summation of where humanity is at can be found in this statement from the Living Planet Report 2018: 'we are the first generation that has a clear picture of the value of nature and the enormous impact we have on it. We may also be the last generation that can act to reverse this trend'. Sobering words indeed, leading many scientists to speak of the Earth as currently experiencing its sixth mass-extinction event.

What Can Be Done to Avert Our Biodiversity Crisis?

The good news is that this trend can be reversed if we, both as individuals and the State, act swiftly and decisively. We now have a better scientific evidence base on ecology and conservation management, so we know what nature needs to survive and prosper. At its simplest level all species require sufficient food resources to stay healthy and in good condition, sufficient good quality habitat in which to shelter and reproduce, and protection from predation and pollution. These resources can be provided in any parcel of land, no matter how small; though clearly the benefits of such actions will only be local.

What Can We as Individuals Do?

Anyone who manages land can take actions that are beneficial for biodiversity. In gardens, planting perennial plants over annuals, reducing the frequency of mowing of lawns to a six-week rotation, and leaving uncut strips or corners for wildlife all help pollinators. Creating a pond, no matter how small, will add huge diversity to any garden through provision of specialised habitat for aquatic life to thrive. Reduction in pesticide use will also be of enormous benefit.

Farmers can have the biggest positive impact on biodiversity. Leaving hedgerows uncut or cut only every three years will allow bushes to blossom and bear fruit, and provide food and nesting habitat for wildlife. The retention of any ponds and not draining wet areas is hugely important for maintaining species diversity. And leaving field margins uncut provides valuable habitat for all types of wildlife. Reduced use of fertiliser would be of enormous benefit.

Local authorities spend huge resources cutting roadside verges and grass in public areas; a simple change in management regime to cut grass in these areas less frequently, and to remove the cutting, would greatly enhance public spaces for wildlife. And those roadside verges that have thin soil covering and often are difficult to cut, should be identified and management specifically for their biodiversity value. This would not only provide huge benefits for biodiversity but it would save money. Public bodies who manage land in their ownership could adopt a similar policy to benefit biodiversity.

What Can the State Do?

While individual piecemeal actions of this type can deliver very important local benefits for biodiversity, the underlying biodiversity crisis cannot be addressed without high-level national leadership on biodiversity, and the introduction of high-level policies to create the conditions for natural ecosystems to function. Such a scenario would have the added benefit of significantly mitigating the worst impacts of climate change on existing land use.

Four policies that would have a huge positive benefit for biodiversity are:

- **Establish a comprehensive network of protected areas**
  On land, designate and conserve a network of sites of national, regional and local importance for nature conservation, supported

by programmes and financial incentives to promote positive land management within these sites. Ireland's semi-natural habitats are so fragmented that, as a matter of urgency, the last remaining fragments of importance at the national, regional and local level must be afforded statutory protection.

In our seas, designate at least 30% of Ireland's inshore waters and 50% of our offshore waters as marine conservation areas where fishing, farming and prospecting would be prohibited. This would ensure that marine biodiversity had a sufficiently large area to flourish and recruit populations to support genuinely sustainable fishing levels elsewhere.

- **Integrate biodiversity management into agricultural management systems**
  All farms in receipt of CAP payments and other subsidies should have a minimum of 20% of their land area actively promoting biodiversity enhancement measures. Aligning farming policy with climate and biodiversity policy is a huge challenge. Recognising and rewarding farmers for positive management of farmland features, including hedgerows, field margins, areas of semi-natural habitats, stream, ponds, etc., would be a very significant step in the right direction.

- **Transition to a forestry programme based solely on native broadleaved species**
  Forest policy needs to transition to a model based on continuous cover native woodland. Phasing out clear-felling of non-native trees on upland peatlands will stop destruction of existing semi-natural habitats and the pollution of our streams and rivers. Planting of Irish species on more appropriate land will have the dual benefit of creating high quality habitat for our native biodiversity and increasing the value of Irish woodland as carbon sinks.

- **Stop destroying Ireland's peatlands to use as fuel**
  In addition to being of inordinate biodiversity value, peatlands are Ireland's most important long-term stores of carbon. All peatlands in public ownership should be transferred to a new state body, Natural Capital Ireland, to safeguard their value and to manage them in the long-term for their natural capital benefits.

Advocacy for Biodiversity within Public Policy

In addition to a robust policy framework, appropriate administrative structures are needed to advocate and deliver public policy. It is somewhat of an anomaly that Ireland doesn't have an independent state agency with responsibility for nature conservation. National Parks and Wildlife Service is the competent authority, but it resides within central government and has no independent identity. The scientific advice it provides to government is hidden from public view, and it never engages in public discourse and consequently Ireland has no champions for biodiversity from within the public sector. A Government Department for Biodiversity and Rural Economy supported by an independent state agency for nature conservation would change that, and give biodiversity a voice around the cabinet table. Its role would be to advocate for biodiversity and to promote innovative ways to demonstrate the benefits of biodiversity to the rural economy and generally work to influence high level decision-making for biodiversity within the public sector. Ireland's biodiversity deserves that, and getting it right will benefit everyone.

Liam Lysaght is the director of the National Biodiversity Data Centre, Ireland.

References

WWF. (2018). *Living Planet Report, 2018: Aiming Higher*. Grooten, M., & Almond, R.E.A. (eds). Switzerland: WWF.

Sánchez-Bayo, F., & Wyckhuys, K.A.G. (2019). 'Worldwide Decline of the Entomofauna: A Review of Its Drivers'. *Biological Conservation*, 232:8–27.

THE WAY FORWARD

WILLIAM O'HALLORAN

Climate Change

The current view on global warming is indisputable and it is extremely likely that the dominant cause is human influence. Observations show that average global temperatures have increased by 0.85°C since 1850 and in recent years these climatic changes have caused impacts throughout the world. Changes in Ireland's climate correspond with global trends. The indications are that climate change will have wide-ranging impacts on Ireland's environment and on human health. Though some uncertainties exist in relation to the extent and rate of future climate change impacts, increasing magnitudes of warming will increase the likelihood of even more severe impacts. There is overall agreement among the scientific community that the negative implications of climate change can be reduced and managed through mitigation and adaptation actions. It would be very unwise for society to read into any uncertainty as an excuse for inaction, which is something that has been happening to date. Though it has taken too long for the issue of climate change to become addressed in Ireland, the good news is that we now have a National Climate Change Adaption Framework and lots of good work is underway. We should not feel powerless to stop climate change, as robust information exists nationally to implement the adaptation actions. This will hopefully lead to increased social, economic and environmental resilience to combat climate change in our country (Department of Communications, Climate Action and Environment, 2018).

Landscape Management to Enhance Biodiversity

Irish people need to become increasingly inspired to help nature. Teaching Irish people about nature in a local sense, so they can better understand the landscape that surrounds and supports them, should make a big difference. Helping nature in local places, at work, at home, or elsewhere will be key to a healthier future.

In the late nineteenth century, an Irish gardener called William Robinson coined the phrase 'the wild garden' and came up with a revolutionary idea when he suggested that the feral beauty of wild plants had a place in what he called 'outside rooms'. Robinson's vision was one where wild plants were allowed to mingle with cultivated ones. His ideas inspired other gardeners throughout Europe (Mabey, 2010). Attitudes have changed in the intervening years and I think it's fair to say that in Ireland we have generally grown to be an intolerant nation when it comes to allowing wild plants to have a place in our gardens and publicly managed green spaces. We often think of the work we do in these spaces as being about maintenance. With weedkillers and lawnmowers, we strive to stop things from growing. We want everything prim, proper, neat and tidy, but that approach can often come at the expense of wild flora. It would be great to see a move back towards a more sympathetic way of managing our landscape. Much like what Robinson had in mind.

Rachel Carson's *Silent Spring* was one of the most influential environmental books of the twentieth century. Carson succeeded in spreading public awareness of the destruction caused through the use of pesticides in the landscape, particularly with regard to serious losses for birdlife (Carson, 1962). Though her work led to some important changes, the message has not been received by everyone. Many Irish people use pesticides without thinking of the consequences of their actions for the health of wildlife and other people. This way of thinking needs to change.

Changes that have occurred in the agricultural landscape have been discussed in terms of areas that are still farmed today. Put simply, we have moved from a non-intensive, high biodiversity farmed landscape to a more intensive, more productive, yet far less biodiversity friendly one. However, there are large tracts of land throughout Ireland along roadsides and in urbanised and industrialised areas that were once, but are no longer, farmland. The farm holdings of the past were free-reigning environments where animals roamed along roadsides and other areas within the farm. In a sense, the entire farm holding was managed by animals. Today, we have created a stricter division between farmed and non-farmed parts of our landscape. Across most of the country, animals such as cows only graze within fenced boundaries. In all of the other parts of the landscape, we are managing and maintaining the remainder of green areas mainly with conventional landscaping and gardening methods. For the most part these methods are not environmentally friendly, because of inappropriate use of chemicals and overuse of noisy and polluting machinery. Examples such as the All-Ireland Pollinator Plan (National Biodiversity Data Centre, 2019), show that there is enormous potential for us to adapt management practices in these no longer farmed green spaces to maximise their benefit for nature.

Making Better Use of Money and Valuing Nature

Healthy ecosystems are the bedrock of a sustainable economy and are essential to the well-being of Irish society. Sometimes we misjudge economic performance and well-being by looking only at income, and not at assets such as biodiversity which help generate this income. The concept of natural capital accounting has advanced in recent years and there is now an internationally agreed method to account for biodiversity resources. The National Biodiversity Plan 2017–2021 is aiming to rectify how finance is sometimes used negatively in Ireland (NPWS, 2017) . For example, how payments to farmers encourage them to convert underutilised areas of land or wild areas into productive farmland, rather than incentivising the farmers to protect and manage these places for wildlife. Evaluating nature conservation interest is a complex process, especially when it comes to subjective value judgements (Institue of Environmental Assessment, 1995).

According to Pádraig Corcoran, an Irish farmer with a passion for nature, agricultural incentives need to take account of the true value of long-established habitats in the farmed landscape. It can take hundreds of years for these habitats to develop and then just hours to wipe them off the map. Pádraig believes that one word, 'ineligibility', has done untold damage to biodiversity in Ireland because areas of land that did not qualify for agricultural subsidies have been cleared away to convert them into eligible productive farmland. This practice results in high nature value habitats being lost, and because many such areas tend to be on poorer quality land, the new eligible farmland created is often not that productive and becomes highly dependent on further subsidies to make it a worthwhile practice for farmers (Corcoran, 2019). How do we evaluate the importance of two-hundred-year-old woodland to a local community? Do we place a value on its importance as an adventure playground for local kids? Should we think of it as a two hundred year down payment on a four-hundred-year-old wood? A new approach to valuing the importance of nature is certainly required.

Include Everyone

Innovation is used to figure out solutions to difficult problems and we will need it to overcome issues associated with the natural environment in Ireland. Enhancing interactions between academia, industry, and government has been fundamentally important in the world of innovation, and it is increasingly recognised that society or local community has also got an important part to play (Carayannis & Campbell, 2012). We have seen the development of 'citizen science' initiatives such as the national Bumblebee Monitoring Scheme (NBDC, 2018). Over one hundred sites are monitored throughout the year by volunteers from the general public and the information gathered is hugely important, not only for endangered bumblebee populations, but also for investigating the effects of landscape use and climate change. Initiatives such as the Bumblebee Monitoring Scheme demonstrate the role that the general public can play in making an important contribution to wildlife conservation. The Wild Work approach referred to earlier is a good example of bringing people together to help people, help nature, help people and another example of how we can work together innovatively can be seen in higher education, where there is a genuine move towards making third-level institutions more civically engaged, so that they can better serve society and vice versa (Irish Universities Association, 2019). We need to integrate everyone in the process of working together to improve society and our environment.

A New Type of Awareness

From my experience, many environmentalists take the view that nature is on the verge of being destroyed, and everything is doomed. Whether we make a comparison with the Ireland of fifty years ago, five hundred years ago or five thousand years ago, scientific evidence will tell us that there has been serious decline in the health of our landscape, a loss of natural habitats and a vanishing of so much of the flora and fauna we have shared this island with. Human behaviour has had a large part to play (Cabot, 1999). We have lost a great deal and we are continuing to do so.

Unfortunately, the natural world has become more abstract to people who live in modern society. If a problem seems too overwhelming, then we bury our heads in the sand. We have developed a poorer societal understanding of the natural cycles in our local landscape. Ecophobia is a fear of ecological deterioration and this so-called fear can contribute to people turning a blind eye to environmental issues (Sobel, 1996). It is thought to be a prevalent issue in environmental education, whereby young people, in particular, are given a burden of responsibility to save the world. A responsibility to rescue species like polar bears and orangutans, who are in dire need because of deforestation, climate change impacts and the destruction we are causing to the places they live in. The problems of the world should not be placed on the shoulders of children and fear-based tactics are perhaps not the best way to encourage the behavioural change required for saving the planet.

The alternative approach is to take a long-term view on how we engage people. Ireland is home to over fifty species of mammal, over four hundred species of birds, over four thousand species of plants and over ten thousand species of insects (Irish Wildlife Trust, 2019). If we share a message of positivity about how fascinating the natural world can be, its resilience, and its importance to us, then over time people will become champions for nature, not because of fear, but because of their genuine appreciation for it.

Finally, we need to address a general trend that has resulted in children and adults alike playing and recreating in more sanitised and so-called safer environments. As a society, we have become afraid to let people experience nature in its purest forms. If someone wants to learn how to rock-climb, they'll think they need to go to an indoor climbing wall first. If someone wants to teach their kids to surf waves, they'll have them develop proficiency for the ocean in a swimming pool. Children no longer build their own tree houses, even though tree-house building has been shown to benefit children in a multitude of ways (Louv, 2005). These examples are just some that I have witnessed. In general, our society has become more artificial in how we live and that's without getting into our use of technological gadgets such as smartphones. Embracing nature in its purest form, up close and personal in your own local environment, can be the antidote for the negative outcomes associated with such changed societal behaviour.

Think Bigger by Thinking Locally

There are messages we sometimes come across, about how little things people do can make a small difference and how this small difference can in turn lead to a greater difference on a larger scale. Maybe even a global scale. This resonates with a story I've been told of a guy who planted a square metre of wildflowers and convinced others to do the same, then metre by metre everyone did their bit until they had created a wonderful ecological corridor for wildlife in their community. If we can recognise that we have the capacity to restore nature in our landscape, especially in places where we may have destroyed much of it, then what's to stop us from doing so? Well, think of it this way: maybe all that's missing is that we have yet to realise just how much we can achieve if we think bigger, think better and think differently in terms of how we value nature and how we would like to live in a more meaningful way with it. The challenge in addressing biodiversity loss and other environmental issues in Ireland is perhaps not as great as what we think. The plight of nature in Ireland is maybe not as hopeless as it may seem. Perhaps the real issue is to do with how we think. If that's the case, then how might we change how we think? Will a change in how we think result in a change in how we act?

It can be easier to comprehend helping nature on a scale such as on a farm, a school, or in a town. In that size of place, it's easier to see how big differences can be made to help improve biodiversity. If the ambition to make a difference is targeted in an area that is smaller in size than the whole country, or even the whole world, then we can certainly achieve results quicker too. Thinking about what can be achieved to help biodiversity on a local scale means setting ourselves locally relevant targets that can be ambitious, but also very achievable in terms of how people feel about being able to succeed in their endeavours.

When we think of nature in a global sense, or even a national sense, it can be difficult for people to comprehend such a scale. Second to that, lofty targets such as saving the planet can increase the chances of becoming demoralised, or thinking you can't really make a difference. If you think about it, saving the planet is a bit too ambitious for most people, yet that is what's being asked of most people. Interestingly, a lot of the actions we are being asked to undertake to save the environment, to halt biodiversity loss and combat climate change are the same actions whether we are asked to help the local environment or indeed the planet. Perhaps it's better to keep the focus on what we can do to help our own country if that, in turn, is going to contribute to saving the planet anyway.

Signs of Hope

In Ireland's Biodiversity Action Plan, the Irish vision for biodiversity is that 'biodiversity and ecosystems in Ireland are conserved and restored, delivering benefits essential for all sectors of society and that Ireland contributes to efforts to halt the loss of biodiversity and the degradation of ecosystems in the EU and globally' (NPWS, 2017).

According to Ireland's EPA, protection of Ireland's remaining wild places from further damage is needed to keep them safe for wildlife and people, both for today and for future generations; and conserving and restoring habitats will protect biodiversity, contribute to public health and well-being and provide significant economic opportunities in areas such as tourism. The EPA sees the need to bring biodiversity into the mainstream through biodiversity action plans, robust monitoring systems, and new approaches like integrating natural capital accounting; to place an economic value on nature in future policies, plans and strategies (Wall, Derham, & O'Mahony, 2016).

In 1986, David Bellamy, a prominent naturalist and TV personality at the time, wrote a beautiful account of Ireland's wild wetland habitats called *Bellamy's Ireland: The Wild Boglands*. Though certainly not the only person to do so, Bellamy wrote that Irish blanket bogs were high on the list of international conservation areas (Bellamy, 1986). He made some sensible recommendations towards preserving and making better biodiversity use of the landscape. Much of the book centres on Bord na Móna, a key stakeholder in terms of the ownership and management of large tracts of Ireland's wetland habitats back then. The organisation owns approximately eighty thousand hectares of land in Ireland today. I remember reading Bellamy's book some ten years ago and thinking how it was a shame that much of what he had said was yet to be realised, but fast forward a few more years and Bord na Móna has announced that by 2030, it will have transitioned from burning peat for power generation into new sustainable businesses such as wind and solar, and they are currently in the process of implementing a biodiversity action plan, a plan which echoes much of what Bellamy had referred to in his message back in the 1980s (Bord na Móna, 2018). To me, the Bord na Móna story gives us hope for the future, and a sense of optimism that sensible ideas do come to fruition eventually.

Power of the People

The current situation in Ireland is that habitat and biodiversity loss are a serious issue and there is an urgent need to develop initiatives to engage society in the decision-making process (Wall, Derham, & O'Mahony, 2016).

Environmental issues have been cast as a political battle between industrialists and environmentalists. We need to reflect on how we can make a living, while also meeting our fundamental needs (Suzuki, 2007). People advocating for change find themselves torn between whether to radically oppose the behaviour of environmentally damaging organisations or to support them in their efforts to change their ways (Torgerson, 1999). We should embrace the idea that most people want to change when they are aware of why and how the change needs to happen.

It's well known that all things are connected in the web of life (Hawley, 1950). However, many of us take it for granted and often forget how each thing in our ecosystem is inextricably linked. I would argue that many modern people are in a lessened state of ecological awareness from living life disconnected from nature; and that this is a factor which results in people disassociating the impact of their own actions on other forms of life. However, there are many positive signs of change in society and there certainly seems to be a societal shift towards genuine action to help the environment.

The younger generation of today will have an impact, politically, on how we care for our landscape in future. Time will tell how impactful they will be, but it's hopeful to think that they will be able to hold sway over our political representatives and that this in turn will lead to the changes that are needed. The likelihood of politics making a positive difference depends on how people interact and understand the landscape around them. Engaging with environmental problems of the world is important, but we also need to engage with the same problems up close in our own community. As well as making decisions with how we vote, we can also make decisions with how we spend. People do need to take responsibility for their own actions, by behaving as responsibly as they can in how they use their money. Buying an organic Irish carrot will have different environmental implications than buying a non-organic carrot from outside this country. Often, the price is the thing we place most importance on, but we need to value things differently.

Maybe we need to reinterpret what it means to be human. We should think of ourselves not as destroyers, but are creators. We can create better places in which we can live more harmoniously with the natural world. Use of natural resources and the need to preserve wilderness are usually seen as two things opposing each other (Torgerson, 1999). We can think in a different way when we begin to imagine what can be done to integrate wildness back into places that have been utilised as resources for other purposes, such as housing, transport and industry.

William O'Halloran is a team leader at Wild Work, a unique initiative with biodiversity at its heart. It supports everyone committed to helping nature and its particular focus is to connect business, biodiversity and local communities. It also supports the work of both local and national organisations involved in the conservation and protection of the natural environment.

References

Bellamy, D. (1986). *Bellamy's Ireland: The Wild Boglands*. Dublin: Country House.

Bord na Móna. (2018). *Bord na Móna Biodiviersity Action Plan*. Available at: https://www.bordnamona.ie/wp-content/uploads/2016/04/Biodiversity-Action-Plan-2016-2021.pdf

Cabot, D. (1999). *Ireland*. London: Harper Collins Publishers.

Carayannis, E.G., & Campbell, D.F. (2012). *Mode 3 Knowledge Production in*

Quadruple Helix Innovation Systems: 21st-Century Democracy, Innovation, and Entrepreneurship for Development. New York: Springer.

Carson, R. (1962). *Silent Spring*. USA: Houghton Mifflin.

Corcoran, P. (2019). *Farming for Nature Podcasts*. Available at: https://www.farmingfornature.ie/resources/podcasts/

Department of Communications, Climate Action and Environment. (2018). *National Adaption Framework: Planning for a Climate Resilient Ireland*. Dublin: Dept. of Communications, Climate Action and Environment.

Hawley, A.H. (1950). *Human Ecology: A Theory of Community Structure*. New York: The Ronald Press Company.

Institute of Environmental Assessment. (1995). *Guidelines for Baseline Ecological Assessment*. London: E & FN Spon.

Irish Universities Association. (2019). *Supporting Higher Education and Society to Work Together*. Available at: http://www. campusengage.ie/

Irish Wildlife Trust. (2019). *Species-list*. Available at: https://iwt.ie/species-list/

Louv, R. (2005). *Last Child in the Woods: Saving Our Children from Nature Deficit Disorder*. New York: Algonquin Books.

Mabey, R. (2010). *Weeds: How Vagabond Plants Gatecrashed Civilization and Changed the Way We Think About Nature*. London: Profile Books Ltd.

National Biodiversity Data Centre. (2019). *Pollinators.ie*. Available at: www.pollinators.ie

NBDC. (2018). *Bumblebee Monitoring*. Available at: http://www.*biodiversityireland.* ie/record-biodiversity/bumblebeemonitoring-scheme/about-the-monitoring-scheme/

NPWS. (2017). *National Biodiversity Plan 2017–2021*. Dublin: Dept. of Culture, Heritage and the Gaeltacht. Available at: https://www.npws.ie/sites/default/files/publications/pdf/National%20Biodiversity%20Action%20Plan%20English.pdf

Sobel, D. (1996). *Beyond Ecophobia: Reclaiming the Heart in Nature Education.* Massachusetts: Orion Society.

Suzuki, D. (2007). *The Sacred Balance: Rediscovering Our Place in Nature*. Vancouver: Greystone Books.

Torgerson, D. (1999). *The Promise of Green Politics*. Durham: Duke University Press.

Wall, B., Derham, J., & O'Mahony, T. (2016). *Ireland's Environment 2016: An Assessment*. Wexford: Environmental Protection Agency.

TRANSPORT FOR SUSTAINABILITY

EAMON RYAN

If we are to live up to the commitment we made in signing the Paris Climate Agreement, we will have to stop burning all fossil fuels by the middle of this century. The scale and speed of that change is without precedent. In a few short decades, we will have to build entirely new energy, food, industrial and transport systems, which provide for the needs of all our people. Making the change will put us at the centre of a new industrial revolution that is starting to take hold across the world. We have an environmental obligation to make the shift but also the very real incentive of changing our economy for the better at the same time.

There are some signs we are limbering up to make the necessary leap. In power generation, we've already taken off, as renewable supplies become cheaper and more reliable by the day. In agriculture, our farmers are also starting to realise the transition could be a positive one. We can better protect farming livelihoods by restoring natural biodiversity and the long-term fertility of our soil.

The public are also increasingly impatient for a new circular economy, particularly when it comes to stopping the single use of plastic. Having spent the last twenty years shipping manufacturing to the east and buying in software from the US, Europe is starting to realise that our future security will best be served by promoting a less wasteful, more social, sustainable and creative local economy. The political story of our time has to be how we implement a green new deal to deliver this just transition.

The one area where the potential for change is still very uncertain, especially in Ireland, is in the transport sector. To date there is no real political support for a switch away from the dominant role played by the private motor car. In our heart of hearts, we appear to still be wedded to some sense of security and comfort that comes from travelling in our own mobile metal cocoon. Even as traffic increases and each individual car gets in the way of the other, we still buy into the advertising dream of finding an open road.

The reality is we are increasingly waiting in vain for the bumper in front of us to move. Unless we change our ways, the gridlock is only going to get worse. The cost of congestion in Dublin is projected to be two billion euro per annum by 2030 and nothing is being done to avert that outcome. Our political system is blind to the problem and continues to buy into the false promise that more roads will unlock the traffic jams. It pays lip service to investing in public transport, while spending twice as much on new roads.

We are sticking to a sprawled form of development, which is the greatest obstacle to the low-carbon transition we need. The National Development Plan, Project Ireland 2040 was agreed in June 2018 without any assessment of the climate implications. It provides for the widening of every motorway approaching Dublin, while at the same time taking out hundreds of urban trees and front gardens to make way for more traffic. Galway is being celebrated as a city of culture, while a new outer orbital motorway will continue the sprawl that is a blight on the city. In Cork, Limerick and Waterford the story is the same; there are proper public transport plans to make them functioning cities.

We now know that the National Development Plan will only deliver at most one third of the carbon reductions we need by 2030 and Project Ireland 2040 shows no vision for how we will meet our longer-term decarbonisation goal. We have to be more ambitious and rethink transport in the same way we are redesigning our energy, agriculture and industrial systems.

Such a change could start with a commitment to taking through traffic out of every town and city centre. The National Planning Framework sets out the right course by recommending we return to having people live within those urban centres. The new Land

Development Agency has been given a brief to find suitable central sites for such housing. They should start by looking at our traditional high streets, where retail businesses are dying as sales switch online and to out-of-town shopping centres. We could revive those streets by promoting new businesses in vacated shop fronts and converting the remainder of the buildings into desirable long-term accommodation.

We should not let the rich architectural heritage in those historic buildings go to ruin. Far better to bring them back to life as new neighbourhoods where one could raise a family. In that way, we could get more efficient use of existing public infrastructure, where people live within walking distance of local schools, shops, churches, playing pitches, cafes and pubs.

We have to reverse the increase in commuting distances that has taken place in Ireland over the last fifty years. Longer times on the road are hindering people's quality of life and undermining a sense of community. If we want to build up our regional cities, then we should invest in public transport that serves their centres, rather than prioritising interurban roads that only promotes more sprawl.

To make this revival work we need to reverse the way in which streets were turned into distributor roads, dominated by cars. We need to insert a new transport hierarchy where pedestrians and cyclists come first, followed by the needs of public transport users. The Bus Connects project in Dublin is a first step in the right direction and we need similar plans for every other city and town in Ireland.

It is not about banning the car, but rather slowing things down and reducing the overall volume of through traffic. We should try to retain local car access and provide for deliveries in a planned way but the current policy of serving as many cars as possible has to change immediately.

In the long run, we should aim to replicate what is happening in Danish cities where they are planning some 50% of all urban trips to be by bike. We could also adopt the Swiss model of guaranteeing a public transport connection to every village above a certain size. In Ireland that will require innovative new bus services, which use digital technologies to allow public transport vehicles meet a range of health, educational, social welfare, postal and other needs.

Lastly we should emulate the Dutch who are planning intercity rail services every fifteen minutes, so the timetable is no longer a big concern. As the country with the least electrified rail network in

Europe we should use the opportunity to upgrade the lines and at the same time widen the tracks. We could then cut our own intercity journey times and provide a similar fast and frequent rail service to the Dutch. If we are serious about tackling climate change we need such ambition. It is not too late to turn things around.

The move to electric vehicles is inevitable because they involve a fraction of the running and maintenance costs of combustion engines. However, what we should not do is just replace one car with the other. Now is the time to switch to a car sharing system where individuals are freed up from having to buy, tax, insure and maintain their own car. Most private cars spend 95% of the time parked, so a shared use ownership model would also free up massive amounts of parking spaces. It would also massively reduce the embodied energy that is involved in the construction and disposal of each car.

When it comes to reducing emissions from flying, land freight and shipping we also need to start thinking outside the box. We could start by reimaging how we sell Ireland as a tourist destination. Rather than being an overnight stop or weekend location, we could promote Ireland as a long-stay vacation destination. Part of the pleasure might be sailing to our shores and tourists would also have time to spread out from our overcrowded cities, to get a real understanding of our people and culture.

By embracing the circular economy, we would also reduce the amount of freight transport in shipping goods and materials over and back across the world. It is not saying no to globalisation but using the latest manufacturing technology to bring production back to the point of use and reuse and repair. Like so many of the other solutions it could involve a leap to a better economic model. One that builds a new sense of community. One that allows us play our part in tackling climate change and at the same time lead out the new industrial revolution.

This should not be a hard sell. We could turn our remoteness into a sustainable advantage. We have a valuable green brand but we need to be good at going green in reality. The climate change challenge is not going to go away. We are better off embracing solutions rather than putting them on the long finger. It is time for our transport system in particular to change.

Eamon Ryan is an Irish Green Party politician who has served as leader of the Green Party since May 2011.

MODERN CULTURE AND WELL-BEING: HOW WE MAY TREAT THE SOCIAL PATHOLOGIES OF CONTEMPORARY CIVILISATION

KIERAN KEOHANE

Global pandemics of anxiety and depression and self-inflected injuries of climate breakdown and species extinction indicate how late-modern civilisation has become, in the words of emergency medicine, 'incompatible with life.' In this short piece, I would like to address the interconnection between health, well-being and human flourishing within the broader context of the value placed on the cultural characteristics of modern society – economism, consumerism, materialism and individualism – and the fact that our modern way of living is becoming unsustainable, with implications for health and for the health of human society in its entirety. In this context, I will suggest what can be done at a personal level as well as at a societal level to make healthy and sustainable life choices.

Suicide; deliberate self-harm; depression; anxiety; obesity, anorexia and bulimia; addictions to alcohol, opioids and other substances; chronic fatigue syndrome on the one hand, and insomnia on the other; stress-related illnesses; psychic pain and distress associated with gender and sexual identities, 'trans' identities, and body dysmorphias; autistic spectrum disorders, attention deficit disorder and hyperactivity; a proliferation of libidinal excesses and compulsions of one form or another –'shopaholics', 'problem gamblers'; malaises related to internet use and social media such as desensitisation to pornography and violence; 'cyber-bullying' and amplifications of envy and rivalry, rage, hate and extremism; loneliness, isolation and despair; 'borderline' conditions such as 'social anxiety disorder' and 'borderline personality disorder'.

These and other conditions present clinically in terms of individualised cases and symptoms, and they have demographic and epidemiological profiles. However, they are represented discretely, as though for the most part unrelated to each other, and they are responded to similarly, each having its own professional discourse of etiology, diagnostics, therapeutics, as well as a task force developing health strategies and policies and interventions. But these contemporary conditions need to be understood in the light of radical changes of social structures and institutions, extending to deep crises in our civilisation as a whole. Problems of health and well-being have hitherto been considered in isolation; both in isolation from one another, and in isolation from broader contexts. But the human person is an indivisible whole, the functioning of the body as an organism is intrinsically linked to the functioning of its mind, and even its 'soul' or 'spirit'. Health and well-being are not just located at the level of the individual body, the integral human person, or even collective social bodies, but encompass the health of humanity as a whole and our relationship with nature. Recovery of our individual and collective health and well-being needs to be conceived of within such a holistic paradigm, encompassing the importance of beauty and meaningfulness to human flourishing.

As well as illnesses that are at least recognised as such, there are more general, diffuse social pathologies of contemporary civilisation that have so far not even been formulated as being problematic. On the contrary, they have come to be seen, broadly, as the normal conditions of life in contemporary society, so much so that, to be sane in a sick society is to be sick relative to the society (Freud, 1961). For instance, under the auspices of the neo-liberal revolution, whereby the norms of society are eclipsed by the principles of the market, a corresponding new type of subject has been emerging. Shaped by the experiences of hyper-individuation and the political-economic and cultural-ideological emphasis on the purported rationality of utility-maximising individual self-interest of *homo economicus* we can see florid symptoms of egoism, conceit, greed and narcissism. Moreover, the amorality of the market and the relativisation and dissolution of collective ethical frameworks and ideals (whether traditional-religious or modern-secular), under conditions of postmodern culture, results in an amplified and intensified anomie and loss of meaningfulness, a moral vacuum experienced individually and collectively. One of the characteristic aspects of this pathogenic milieu is a generalised experience of liminality, a sense of being neither here nor there but betwixt and between, a morbid interregnum wherein we are stuck in a moment so to speak; living in an interminable present, with a lack of sense of history on the one hand and lack of a sense of a future, other than an extension of the present, on the other. Characteristic social pathologies of this condition of 'permanent liminality' include, for instance: an acceleration and intensification of sensations (rather than meaningful experiences); a proliferation of choices (rather than significant decisions); and individual and collective amnesia and aphasia corresponding with loss of historicity; and of despair and hopelessness corresponding with loss of futurity (Szakolczai, 1998).

The most generalised pathology of contemporary civilisation is what the Greeks called 'pleonexia'. Pleonexia is excessive and insatiable greed, vaulting ambition and envy combined with extreme social inequality and distributive unfairness of money, power, esteem and of all divisible social goods. Three millennia of religious, ethical, philosophical, political and even medical discourse identify pleonexia as pathological, as being *the* problem of the classical city, paradigmatically Athens, where its greatest minds – Socrates, Plato and Aristotle – all identify it as the cause of the collapse of civilisation, a theme repeated by the historians Thucydides and Livy in the case of the decline and fall of Rome. But neoliberalism makes a virtue of pleonexia – 'greed is good'! Pleonexia is always latent, as it is anchored in human appetites and desires, but it becomes a manifest problem only under particular conditions. Ordinarily managed and mediated within the collective morality, pleonexia becomes a problem at times of historical, social and political change and transformation. People tend to become extravagantly acquisitive, over-reaching in their ambitions, suspicious and aggressively envious of others when the normal constraints and limits that govern individual appetites and desires are loosened and become uncertain. Pleonexia cannot be contained when there is no certainty, no consensus on the limiting principles according to which distribution should take place. In such circumstances 'the powerful do what they can, and the weak suffer what they must' (Thucydides, 1972/431BCE; Thucydides is citing the justification given by the Athenians for the massacre of Melos, one of the first recorded war crimes).

Pathologies of contemporary civilisation should be comprehended as multiple and as being related to one another, and as not merely problems to be understood and addressed at the level of the individual sufferer but rather as to be understood in social and historical terms, for 'neither the life [or the health] of an individual nor the history of a society can be understood without understanding both' (Wright Mills, 1959). Instead of addressing these conditions as though they were discrete pathologies – specific diseases suffered by private individuals as 'cases' – the starting point should be that the sources of these illnesses and malaises are social, cultural, and historical: that they arise from collectively experienced conditions of social transformations and shifts in our civilisation. These diagnostics of social pathologies of contemporary civilisation also suggest corresponding therapeutics. When we consider the challenges of recovery we realise that our individual and collective health and well-being will require more than changes at the level of the discourse of professional medicine, or at the level of public health services and policies, but, more fundamentally, a revitalisation of our social, political, cultural and moral institutions.

The methods and mindsets of modernity are fully implicated in the malaises of our times, from existential threats of climate breakdown and species extinction to the insidious and pervasive dissolution of traditions, values, ideals, and holistic mythopoetic consciousness as sources of meaningfulness, limit horizons and models to emulate. Modern life comes at the price of disenchantment, fragmentation, a dearth of good models and loss of a sense of coherence that is essential to health, well-being and human flourishing. In *The Future Public Health,* Hanlon and colleagues say that we are confronted with 'a yawning gulf between the problems we face and our capacity to think up workable solutions', a gulf that has been dubbed the 'myth gap' (Hanlon, Carlisle, Hannah, & Lyon, 2011).

The scale of the problems that we face is so enormous (pandemic depression afflicting three hundred million, costing two hundred billion dollars a year; an overheating planet and global climate breakdown) their sources are so abstract (the growth imperative of global capitalism; the acceleration and simultaneous decline of modern civilisation) and our political structures and systems of governance operate at such a remove from ordinary people and everyday life that we find ourselves feeling alienated and powerless, and this leaves us vulnerable to populist demagogues who promise to 'give us back our country' and 'make us great again' while stirring up even more chaos.

In this context, what can be done at a personal level as well as at a societal level to make healthy and sustainable life choices?

If we liken the modern world to a huge machine accelerating wildly and about to crash, we can imagine some minor adjustments that we could make that would change its whole direction. Such small changes that can bring about great transformations include, for instance: moving away from meat and dairy towards a vegetable based diet. Not alone is a meat and dairy-based diet strongly implicated in obesity, heart disease, orthopaedic problems, cancers, as well as antibiotics resistance at the level of individual health and illness, the meat and dairy industry is the second biggest cause (after fossil fuel consumption) of global warming, deforestation and freshwater pollution. Furthermore, the meat and dairy industry is morally and spiritually corrosive insofar as it rests upon and perpetuates a culture of animal cruelty and insensitivity to suffering. If one were to do one small thing to improve their own personal health and the health and well-being of the whole planet – something that is entirely within the reach of one's own personal agency – then avoiding meat and dairy in favour of a vegetarian diet is that one small step.

The next small step is to walk. Our sedentary lifestyle is at the root of much loss of health and well-being, so public health education promotes exercise, typically running. Running is fine, but insofar as it encourages people to buy into imperatives of competition, taking up 'challenges' of one sort or another, even competing against one's own 'personal best', running feeds into and amplifies the culture of individualism and perpetual competitiveness that underpins many of the wider sources of the malaises and sicknesses of our current civilisation. Walking, on the other hand, is not only a greatly undervalued form of physical exercise, walking is a truly human and re-humanising experience (Szakolczai & Horvath, 2017;

O'Neill & Hubbard, 2010). The pace of walking is a human rhythm, and it is a sociable and convivial rhythm that facilitates and enables companionship and conversation; and equally walking facilitates solitude, quietness, thinking and reflection. Walking decelerates an over-accelerated world, and when we adopt a slower pace the world discloses itself to us in entirely new ways so that we can begin to attune to others and to our surroundings and become mindful of beauty in nature and harmony and gracefulness in the ordinary and everyday.

Walking may be the first step towards re-orienting our lives towards an elevated horizon of meaningful ideals. 'Meaningful ideals' may seem intangible, impractical and inconsequential, but in fact they are absolutely essential. Human life is oriented towards something more than biological imperatives of survival and reproduction: human beings *lead* our lives; we are led by the light of ideals; and human life is life that follows: life that follows causes and callings. These are the sources of coherence and meaningfulness in human life, and 'striving to find a meaning in one's life is the primary motivational source in man' (Frankl, 1959).

Focus, purpose, rhythm, elevation, and limit horizons are essential for joyful, healthy and hopeful life. Historically and anthropologically people and societies are only healthy while they have a generally shared limit horizon of transcendent ideals and a mythopoetic cosmology or 'spirituality'. It is only by virtue of elevating ideals of beauty and truth that we can focus purposefully on the good life, and may find meaningful answers to the perennial and ultimate questions of human existence: 'How should we live?' 'What is the meaning of life?' and 'Is there an afterlife?'

The collapse of civilisations, whether in Mesopotamia, Greece, Rome, and the civilisations of the Orient and pre-Columbian Americas were all preceded by confusion of ideals and decline in the authority of their various gods. Modern western civilisation is no exception. Since the beginning of the modern age, starting with the Enlightenment just two hundred years ago (a very short time in the arc of humanity), we are a civilisation dedicated to an ideal of 'progress' to be achieved by breaking limits: 'Just Do It' and 'No Fear' are amongst our brands and watchwords. Progress entails throwing down the old gods and idols while simultaneously elevating and proclaiming new 'names of the Father' to replace them: 'Reason' and 'Science'; the 'Nation', the 'People' and the 'Party'; 'Fuhrers' and

'Great Leaders' of one sort or another; and presently 'the invisible hand' of the purportedly omniscient and omnipotent 'Market' have all served as transcendent sources of authority (Dufour, 2008). Today these authorities are all confused and confusing: facts are countered by 'alternative facts'; nothing and no one is trusted, not even life-preserving vaccines. Short-term contracts, ever-changing projects and 'flexibilisation' replace stable, secure occupational and professional vocations. Secularism clashes with new fundamentalisms; hedonistic libertarian hyper-individualism vies with fatalism, despair and nihilism. These swirling social currents are related to the great waves of anxiety, depression and pleonexia that are the epidemics of our time.

How might we find the meaningfulness and sense of coherence that are essential to joyful and hopeful life amidst such conditions? Paradoxically, we might find it by paying attention to mortality. Mortality, the fact that we shall all die, is the one thing that is certain in life, and it is the thing that modern society especially tries to deny by our cult of eternal youth and the many ways we try to distract ourselves from the inevitability of our death. Our present age lacks an *Ars Moriendi*, an 'art of dying', save for the remnants of Judaeo-Christian legacy augmented by scraps borrowed from the patrimony of world religions. We spend our lives distracting ourselves from the Void by amusing and consuming ourselves to death, whereas we could follow the advice of Montaigne who says 'let us converse and become familiar with death' (Montaigne, 1993/1580). We should become conversant and familiar with death because 'the tacit presence of mortality in everyday life acts as a limit horizon that gives form and meaning to life' (Blum, 2016). Modern civilisation ignores and denies human limits at the cost of anthropological grounds of sustainable life on the one hand and transcendent ideals on the other. By lacking resonant relations between grounds and limits, life becomes incoherent and minds become unstrung. If we want to learn how we may live a right life, even when our time is wrong, then in these end times we should visit the sick, care for the dying, and bury the dead.

Kieran Keohane is the head of the Department of Sociology, University College Cork. Research interests include: Social pathologies of contemporary civilisation; effects of anomie and liminality on health, well-being and human flourishing.

References

Blum, A. (2016). *The Dying Body as a Lived Experience*. London: Routledge.

Dufour, D.R. (2008). *The Art of Shrinking Heads: On the New Servitude of the Liberated in an Age of Total Capitalism*. Cambridge: Polity Press.

Frankl, V. (1959). *Man's Search for Meaning*. Boston: Beacon Press.

Freud, S. (1961). *Civilization and its Discontents*. New York: Norton & Co.

Hanlon, P., Carlisle, S., Hannah, M., & Lyon, A. (2011). *The Future Public Health*. Berkshire: Open University Press.

de Montaigne, M. (1993) [1580]. 'That to Study Philosophy is to Learn to Die'. *The Complete Essays*. London: Penguin Classics.

O'Neill, M., & Hubbard, P. (2010). 'Walking, Sensing, Belonging: Ethno-mimesis as Performative Praxis'. *Visual Studies*, 25(1): 46–58.

Szakolczai, A. (1998). *Reflexive Historical Sociology*. London: Routledge.

Szakolczai, A., & Horvath, A. (2017). *Walking into the Void: A Historical Sociology and Political Anthropology of Walking*. London: Routledge.

Thucydides. (1972) [431BCE]. *The History of the Peloponnesian War*. Finley, M.I. (trans.). London; Penguin Classics.

Wright Mills, C. (1959). *The Sociological Imagination*. Oxford: Oxford University Press.

THE WAY FORWARD IN THE BEST OF TIMES AND THE WORST OF TIMES

IVAN J. PERRY

Reflecting on modern culture from the perspective of health and well-being, one is reminded of the opening line from Charles Dickens's *A Tale of Two Cities*, set at the time of the French Revolution in 1789, 'It was the best of times, it was the worst of times, it was the age of wisdom, it was the age of foolishness ...' Over the past century we have seen marked improvements in longevity, health and well-being in developed, high-income countries worldwide with increasing wealth and profound improvements in social and economic conditions. In Ireland, we have seen the virtual eradication of major causes of death from infectious disease in childhood, massive improvements in maternal and child health, significant reductions in deaths and injuries from road traffic accidents and substantial declines in death rates from stroke and coronary heart disease, especially in young and middle-aged adults. We spend more on our health service than ever before and we can now treat conditions that in the past would have led to death or enduring misery. Ireland is currently ranked fourth in the UN's Human Development Index, a composite index of life expectancy, education, and per capita income indicators. There is also evidence of positive cultural changes in recent decades in our understanding and tolerance for diversity and human frailty. In particular, a subtler appreciation of the psychological vulnerability of children and adolescents and a greater capacity than heretofore to address difficult social, emotional and psychological issues is evident in our public discourse. Alongside these positive indicators of the best of times, there are of course issues of concern, a sense of the worst of times. In Ireland, as in other developed countries, we have high rates of obesity in children and adults which are likely to stall and potentially reverse the recent declines in stroke and coronary heart disease mortality and lead to increased rates of diabetes, cancer and a range of other conditions that will increase demand for health services. Despite the high levels of expenditure on health services, media discussion on health is enveloped in a sense of perpetual crisis and scarcity with public dismay at long waiting times, sub-standard care, staff shortages and financial mismanagement. We are experiencing increasing rates of alcohol and other drug misuse, increasing rates of mental distress in young people and there are significant and troubling social inequalities in health that begin in early childhood and extend across the life course to old age. The latter issue – that of social inequalities in health related to wealth and social status – is of particular concern. For example, although average life expectancy at birth in Ireland in 2019 has risen to eighty-two years, in the Travelling Community it is estimated at sixty-two years. Indeed, when we study different groups in the population, whether defined by the distribution of educational attainment, wealth, income, occupational status or by area of residence we see clear and consistent differences in health and well-being across these distributions, reflecting the gradations in access to the power, money and other resources that ultimately determine our health and well-being.

Unfortunately, when we take a wider, global or planetary health perspective, the *worst of times* and *the age of foolishness* come into even sharper focus, as we consider a series of interlinked problems that pose both profound threats to the health and well-being of populations in the twenty-first century and fundamental challenges to the existing political and economic world order. We are stretching critical planetary boundaries that define the Earth's safe operating space with accelerating greenhouse gas emissions and global warming, species extinction and loss of biodiversity and the profligate abuse of finite resources including freshwater and croplands, all driven by an increasing global population that is projected to reach ten billion by the year 2050 (Willett, Rockström, Loken et al., 2019). These core threats to the fragile ecosystem that sustains life on our planet are related to each other and to a series of additional problems that affect all countries and regions at some level but bear most heavily on lower and middle income countries. Nine out of ten people on our planet breathe polluted air every day, leading to seven million premature deaths per annum. We are experiencing a pandemic of obesity and non-communicable diseases (including heart disease, stroke, diabetes and cancer) propagated via the global promotion of processed food, sedentary lifestyles and tobacco smoking. There are ongoing and emerging epidemics of infectious disease involving new and old pathogens such as Ebola and Tuberculosis, the ever-present possibility of a global influenza pandemic and an alarming rise in resistance to commonly prescribed antimicrobials. It is estimated that more than 1.6 billion people (22% of the global population) are currently without access to basic shelter, nutrition, security and care due to a combination of challenges and crises, including drought, famine, conflict, population displacement and weak health services.

It is of course easier to define the challenges to health, well-being and sustainability that we face on this small, interconnected and interdependent planet than it is to identify solutions. It may be helpful first to consider briefly what we can learn from the past, from the history of public health in particular, before we consider our present situation and how we might chart a way forward.

From the most cursory survey of the history of public health since the Enlightenment, it is difficult to avoid the conclusion that each generation needs to learn the same basic lesson that health and well-being are determined primarily by political and social factors that influence the distribution of power and resources in society and that the role of the health sector is essentially marginal (Porter, 1997). Many historical figures have highlighted the extent to which social pathology drives human pathology – from Frederick Engels who wrote about the condition of the working class in England in 1845 to Salvador Allende (Minister of Health and later president of Chile until his death in a right-wing military coup in 1973) who refused to discuss specific health problems apart from macro-level political and economic issues. However, it was the great German pathologist and polymath Rudolf Virchow who provided the clearest and most direct expression of the political, social and economic determinants of health and well-being with his much quoted but largely ignored statement: 'Medicine is a social science and politics is nothing else but medicine on a large scale.' In his report on the 1848 Typhus outbreak in upper Silesia (now part of Poland), he wrote that:

> ... free and unlimited democracy is the single most important principle. If we get free and well-educated people, then we shall undoubtedly have healthy ones as well ... The task of any reasonable and democratic government will always be to educate the people and liberate them, not only materially but spiritually ...

While the health sector provides a vital resource and safety net when we are concerned about our health, when we are sick and when we are dying, it is now time to move the discourse on health and well-being beyond the narrow confines of the clinical arena. We also need to move beyond what has been described as the 'lazy language of lifestyle' that emerged towards the latter end of the twentieth century and has been adopted uncritically by health professionals, policymakers, the media and the general public (de Gruchy, 2019). The term 'lifestyle' frames health and well-being at an individual level – effectively blaming individuals for making irrational decisions that are detrimental to their health. As we face a series of interconnected challenges that imperil life on Earth and demand profound system level change at government and inter-governmental level, the language of lifestyle perpetuates a disproportionate focus on the need for individuals to make different choices and changing their 'unhealthy lifestyle'. While it would be good if all of us in Ireland could switch off the lights in our homes and offices when we can, drive an electric car and eat less meat, it is clear that for meaningful progress toward reducing our greenhouse gas emissions we need to stop burning coal and peat in our power stations as quickly as possible and develop policies that will effectively reduce our national beef and dairy herds.

In *The Future Public Health*, published in 2012, Phil Hanlon – a public health physician who spent his working life addressing the health and well-being of the people of Glasgow – and colleagues argue that although the modern era that emerged from the scientific revolution and the Enlightenment in the seventeenth century has brought many advantages that have transformed life on Earth for the better, there are cultural characteristics of modern society (embedded in the DNA of the enlightenment) that now pose significant threats to our health and well-being (Hanlon, Carlisle, Hannah, & Lyon, 2011). In particular, he highlights the inter-related issues of economism, materialism and consumerism and an over-emphasis on individualism. The notion of economism refers to the tendency to view the world primarily through the lens of economics and to prioritise short-term economic considerations above our long-term interests and wider human values. This is linked to materialism and consumerism – the expectation of constant and ever-increasing economic growth, regardless of the impact on the environment or the depletion of finite resources; and the tendency to search for meaning, happiness and fulfilment through consumption. While the priority now accorded to individualism, freedom and human rights is a significant positive feature of the modern era, an over-emphasis on individualism blinds us to the fundamental reality of our interconnection and interdependence with all life on Earth. In language reminiscent of Virchow's focus on the need for both 'material' and 'spiritual' liberation Hanlon points a way forward. Drawing on Plato, he argues that in our current efforts to promote the health and well-being of populations we tend to focus too much on science (the true) at the expense of the beautiful (aesthetics) and the good (ethics). This is not an argument that diminishes the importance of reason and science. Indeed, in the current era of science denialism and shameless propaganda from corporate-vested interests on issues such as processed food and climate change we need to defend the values of the enlightenment – the need to separate (insofar as possible) fact from opinion and science from ideology. Unfortunately, however, science and reason will not be enough if we are to successfully engage with the 'wicked', context dependent problems that imperil health, well-being and sustainability in the twenty-first century. In the particular example of climate change it is clear that the detailed and scientifically rigorous reports from the Inter-Governmental Panel on Climate Change (IPCC) have not been enough to move hearts and minds on the need for radical change to reduce greenhouse gas emissions.

It is increasingly clear that if we are to limit the harms from climate change and promote health, well-being and human flourishing, we need broadly based movements that are grounded in science but with the capacity to engage individuals and communities at the level of the beautiful and the good. To some extent this is already happening in response to the now imminent threats of uncontrolled greenhouse gas emissions, as evidenced by the resurgence of Green politics and related movements in Europe and the proposed 'Green New Deal' in the United States. Public health needs to be at the forefront of these movements, deeply engaged at all levels with social, economic and political activism that seeks to acknowledge and celebrate the beauty and fragility of our planet and cultivate a popular narrative or moral consensus focused on justice, compassion and interdependence within and across generations and with all life on Earth. There are particular opportunities for public health as a participant in broadly based movements for planetary health, sustainability and human flourishing to highlight (in the manner of Virchow in 1848) the profound and almost immediate effects on health and well-being of moving towards an ecologically sustainable society, rooted in environmentalism, non-violence, social justice, grassroots democracy and a truly liberating education system.

Movement in the direction of an ecologically sustainable society may not be beyond us if we can address what Alex Evans has described as the 'Myth Gap' (Evans, 2017). Evans is a contemporary climate change and development policy analyst who has worked at intergovernmental Group of Eight (G8) level. He reminds us that evidence and arguments are much less important than values in determining our approach to social and political issues and that values are in turn shaped by stories or myths. He defines myths as stories that help us to understand the world and ourselves and he argues that a core element in the current success of populist leaders in Britain, the US and elsewhere is their ability to speak to the contemporary absence of – and deep hunger for – grand narratives or myths that explain 'where we are, how we got here, where we might be trying to get to, and underneath it all who we are'. Evans argues that we now need myths that change how we see our place in the world ('a larger us'), shift how we see our place in time ('a longer now') in which we get back to thinking in generational timespans, and a different model of progress ('a different version of the good life') in which growth is less a story of increasing material consumption and more about us finally growing up as a species.

This is undoubtedly a challenging agenda, but it is realistic and achievable when we consider how far we have come in the promotion of health and well-being on this planet. The way forward will require us to promote diversity, innovation and deep freedom in our social and political enterprises and ultimately tap into the indomitable human spirit to survive and flourish (Unger, 2014). In these best of times and worst of times, this is surely not beyond us.

Ivan J. Perry is professor of public health in the School of Public Health, University College Cork.

References

de Gruchy, J. (2019). 'The Lazy Language of "Lifestyles": Let's Rid This from Our Talk About Prevention'. The Association of Directors of Public Health (ADPH). Available at: https://www.adph.org.uk/2019/04/the-lazy-language-of-lifestyleslets-rid-this-from-our-talk-about-prevention

Evans, A. (2017). *The Myth Gap: What Happens When Evidence and Arguments Aren't Enough?*. London: Penguin Books.

Hanlon, P., Carlisle, S., Hannah, M., & Lyon, A. (2011). *The Future Public Health*. Berkshire: Open University Press.

Porter, R. (1997). *The Greatest Benefit to Mankind: A Medical History of Humanity from Antiquity to the Present*. W.W. Norton & Company.

Unger, R.M. (2014). *The Religion of the Future*. Cambridge: Harvard University Press.

Willett, W., Rockström, J., Loken, B., Springmann, M., Lang, T., Vermeulen, S., ... & Jonell, M. (2019). 'Food in the Anthropocene: The EAT–Lancet Commission on Healthy Diets from Sustainable Food Systems'. *The Lancet*, 393(10170), 447–492. Available at: https://doi.org/10.1016/S0140-6736(18)31788-4

OPENING PANDORA'S BOX

FRED POWELL

> In my humble study I am most virtuous ...
> I strum my plain old zither, read Buddhist sutra,
> No music to grate my ears
> No office to tire my mind and soul.

'My Humble Study' by Liu Yuxi (772–847 CE)

Liu Yuxi's poetic words written nearly two thousand years ago resonate down the centuries. He was a philosopher, poet and consummate administrator, whose life balanced thought and action. That is the essential point in the poem. It looks like the twenty-first century will be the Chinese century. Therefore, it is important to understand Chinese culture in order to unlock our future in the same manner that American culture explains our present and European culture our past. Liu Yuxi's imagery captures the importance of reflection in a turbulent world that rejects the metaphysical in favour of consumerist satisfaction. Ayn Rand, the author of choice of many American students, in her influential novels *Atlas Shrugged* and *The Fountainhead* promotes the virtue of 'ethical egoism' in her anarcho-capitalist vision of the future.

Arguably, if the world is to remain a sustainable planet, fit for human habitation, it will need citizens to produce a counter narrative of an ethical civil society, based on civic virtue, social justice and democracy. This is Karl Polanyi's theory of 'double movement' – a titanic struggle between the push for self-regulating markets and the push back for social rights, multiculturalism and democracy – as the ingredients of a sustainable future society.

Opening Pandora's Box

The phrase 'hope springs eternal' is derived from a poem written by Alexander Pope in 1733 called 'An Essay on Man'. The theme underpinning the poem is the fortitude of humanity in always finding a reason for hope in the future. Pope was celebrated by contemporary philosophers, notably Rousseau and Voltaire, for his optimistic belief in humanity. In fact, the virtue of hope has featured from the start of civilisation. The Ancient Greek poet Hesiod, who lived around the same time as Homer between 750 and 650 BCE, wrote the myth of Pandora's Box that has resonated down the millennia. The story is commonly viewed as a dark myth that warns against curiosity because it challenges the power of the gods. In reality, it is a narrative of human liberation. Pandora is entrusted with a box, which she opens, defying the commandments of the gods. Out fly evil spirits leading to dire warnings ever since against the dangers of opening Pandora's box. However, Hesiod's original version of the Pandora myth has an entirely different meaning. According to Hesiod's version, at the bottom of the box is a good spirit called hope! Hope in the future is arguably the fundamental inspiration that drives humanity.

The parallels between Hesiod's Pandora's Box and the biblical story of Adam and Eve eating the famous apple from The Tree of Knowledge are unmistakable. Eve's incitement to Adam to eat the apple from the Tree of Knowledge is a metaphor. By eating the apple Adam is seeking to make himself omniscient like God. In response an outraged God banishes Adam and Eve from the Garden of Eden, as the eternal punishment of humanity for the offence of seeking equality of knowledge with the divinity – the 'original sin' that led to the fall of humanity.

The moral in the story of Adam and Eve is quite dark. It conflicts with the project of modernity, which is driven by a transformative vision of the future. We call it human progress. In a secular age, citizens subscribe to the adage 'Knowledge will set you free'. A core belief in contemporary civilisation is that knowledge is the key to unlocking the future. Arguably, knowledge is the last best hope of civilisation. That is why we search for greater knowledge about our world through scientific exploration and invention on the one hand and philosophical speculation on the other, in the hope of changing human existence for the better and ultimately rediscovering paradise. However, historical experience tells us that knowledge without civic virtue can lead to a catastrophic world. The Ancient Greek philosopher Plato promoted a vision of a utopian society ruled by 'philosopher kings' in his most famous work *The Republic.* Unfortunately, tyranny was inherently embedded in this idealised society. In acknowledgement of this existential reality, Plato produced his 'second best' model for society in two subsequent works *The Statesman* and *The Laws.* The Ancient Greeks had discovered there is no paradise on Earth and only an ethical civil society based on civic virtue works. They called it democracy.

Civic Virtue and Civil Society

In the debate about civil society key concepts – citizenship, community, participative democracy – all originate in the Ancient Greek world. The *agora* (public square or market place) became both the symbolic and real embodiment of the space where democracy happened. It was underpinned by the right to associate, which was revived during the Velvet Revolutions of the late twentieth century that peacefully overthrew tyrannies in Eastern and Southern Europe. During the twenty-first century we have witnessed the Arab Spring, which has struggled to bring democracy to the Maghreb-Mashreq region. In the liberal democratic world we have also witnessed citizen action movements on the streets in the form of the Occupy Movement, *Los Indignados* and latterly the *Gilets Jaunes* (Yellow Vests) in France. These movements are manifestations of a political dimension of civil society that harnesses the power of street politics and direct action (socially constructed as 'the people') to contest the power of elites (Powell, 2007).

In social realty, civil society has diverse dimensions that encompass both the public and private spheres of life. Civil society in public discourse is frequently equated with the voluntary and community sectors. However, the concept of civil society also encompasses the family, churches, clubs and societies that are at the heart of popular culture (e.g. The GAA). We value civil society because we see it as the expression of civic virtue in our fragile civilisation. Thomas Paine, the author of *The Rights of Man,* advocated the importance of civil society by renaming it 'civilised society' (Paine, 2011). Whatever its name, civil society is synonymous with civic virtue.

The Circle of Life

A Chinese student recently gave me a poem that philosophically captures the existential importance of civic virtue in the life of the citizen, if it is to have a moral basis:

Karma

When a bird is alive, it eats ants.
When the bird is dead,
Ants eat the bird.

Time and circumstances
Can change at any time.
Don't devalue or hurt anyone in life.
You may be powerful today,
But remember,
Time is more powerful than you.
One tree makes a million match sticks
But only one match is needed
To burn a million trees.
So be good and do good.

(*Buddhist Journal,* 14 November 2018)

Civil Society, Apocalyptic Times and the Hope of Humanity

The welfare state has offered social protection to the citizen from 'the cradle to the grave'. It repositioned the state towards civil society in a project driven by the ideal of civic virtue. Globalisation and the marketisation of society has undermined the welfare state at its foundations. The distinguished sociologist Zygmunt Bauman has analysed globalisation and its discontents that in his view are undermining social solidarity, the nation state and our sense of community. In what Bauman calls 'liquid modernity' hyper-development has put the global market beyond political regulation and democratic accountability. The Ancient Chinese expression, 'may you live in interesting times', captures the historical moment of our times.

Slavoj Žižek in his apocalyptic book *Living in the End Times* (2011) offers a challenging vision of the present world order, arguing that the Four Horsemen of the Apocalypse have arrived in the form of a worldwide ecological crisis; imbalances within the economic system; the biogenetic revolution and exploding social divisions and ruptures. Francis Fukuyama had already somewhat hubristically claimed in his bestselling book *The End of History* (1992) that the great ideological debates of the previous two centuries were over and liberal democracy had won! Others were more sceptical. The Japanese philosopher Takeshi Umehara, observed that the collapse of communism was only the precursor of the collapse of liberal democracy. The two grand narratives of the European Enlightenment were doomed in his jaundiced view. The rise of populist politics, exemplified by the election of Donald Trump as US president and the EU/UK Brexit saga, suggests something is seriously wrong with liberal democracy. The financial crash of 2008 underlines the fragility of Western democracy in its current neoliberal form and the need for new and more inclusive democratic forms that foreground civil society.

Bertolt Brecht, the great German poet and playwright, captured the dilemma we face in relation to a civil society based on civic virtue in a poem:

A Bed for the Night

I hear that in New York
At the corner of 26th street and Broadway
A man stands every evening during the winter
  months
And gets beds for the homeless there
By appealing to passers by

It won't change the world
It won't improve relations among men
It will not shorten the age of exploitation
But a few men have a bed for the night
For a night the wind is kept from them
The snow meant for them falls on the
  roadway.

Don't put down the book on reading this, man.

A few people have a bed for the night
For the night the wind is kept from them
The snow meant for them falls on the roadway
But it won't change the world
It won't improve relations among men
It will not shorten the age of exploitation

Bertolt Brecht (1931)

This simple poem about the Great Depression starts a conversation about the relationship between altruism and social change. Should we be glad 'a few men have a bed for the night' or despairing that 'it will not shorten the age of exploitation'? The answer depends on how you read the poem and is ultimately shaped by your own concept of civic virtue.

Conclusion

Pandora's box is already open. Should we be despairing? Or do we see hope in the future lurking at the bottom of Pandora's box? The answer really depends on how we view the world. Do we understand it as a place condemned to eternal misery following the fall of humankind? Or do we believe that through civic virtue it is possible to create a decent society, based on the values of social justice and equality? Hope must be our inspiration for the future because without it we have no purpose. Hope in Hesiod's poem (reputedly the first poem) is salvation.

Fred Powell served as head of the School of Applied Social Studies at University College, Cork, from 1989–2014. His research interests incorporate the exploration of civil society and a socially inclusive view of citizenship from a variety of perspectives, both social, political and philosophical.

References

Fukuyama, F. (1992). *The End of History*. New York: Free Press.

Paine, T. (2011). *Rights of Man*. Grogan, C. (ed.). London: Broadview Press.

Powell, F.W. (2007). *The Politics of Civil Society: Neoliberalism or Social Left?*. Bristol: Policy Press.

Žižek, S. (2011). *Living in the End Times*. New York: Verso.